Shetland Rambles

ART RAMBLES
IN
SHETLAND.

BY JOHN T. REID.

" Here rise no groves, and here no gardens blow,
Here even the hardy heath scarce dares to grow ;
But rocks on rocks, in mist and storm array'd,
Stretch far to sea their giant colonnade.
With many a cavern seam'd, the dreary haunt
Of the dun seal and swarthy cormorant,
Wild, round their rifted brows with frequent cry,
As of lament, the gulls and gannets fly,
And from their sable base, with sullen sound,
In sheets of whitening foam the waves rebound."—SCOTT.

EDINBURGH: EDMONSTON AND DOUGLAS.
1869.

Shetland Rambles

A SKETCHING TOUR OF SHETLAND
RETRACING THE FOOTSTEPS OF
VICTORIAN ARTIST JOHN T. REID

Mairi Hedderwick

BIRLINN

Ma's briag bhuam e, is briag h-ugam e

If it be a lie from me, it's a lie to me

First published in
Great Britain in 2011 by

Birlinn Ltd
West Newington House
10 Newington Road
Edinburgh
EH9 1QS

www.birlinn.co.uk

ISBN: 978 1 84158 998 5

British Library Cataloguing-in-Publication Data
A catalogue record for this book is available
on request from the British Library

Typeset and designed by Mark Blackadder

Printed and bound in Britain by Gutenberg Press, Malta

To the Bonxies

Contents

Foula

Foreword

'He wrote and illustrated a book about Shetland, too, you know . . .'

It was this chance remark by the archivist in Lerwick library that planted the seeds for this book. Douglas Sinclair knew that I had previously written and illustrated a contemporary version of John T. Reid's 1878 *Art Rambles in the Highlands and Islands*.

On sighting that book for the first time, I was immediately attracted to the engravings accompanying the text. Would the views be the same after all those years? And having a somewhat stubborn yet romantic streak, I determined to find out by faithfully following Reid's routes, finding his vantage points and then replicating each view, with the added advantage of full colour reproduction.

That was ten years ago.

Never did I think I would be doing the same thing once again. *Art Rambles in Shetland* could not be ignored. Here was an opportunity to explore Shetland with a familiar mentor.

He was obviously a younger man in 1867 travelling through Shetland than his older self rambling in the Highlands and Islands in 1876. The irony is that the sum total of both his ages on those two prodigious walking tours is much less than my own, shall I say, mature years. But I kept up with him. Not on the horse, however.

I sometimes wish I had found the Shetland book first, as here was a travelling companion much more to my liking.

The older Mr Reid had a missionary zeal that could cloud our conversation on occasion. He greatly irritated me. Subsequent to the latter book, he answered the 'Call for a Hundred Missionaries for China'. He married one of the co-respondents and died in the province of Kiangsi in 1917.

His Shetland *Rambles* do not evangelise, except in the sense of his need to share '*the grander and wilder things in scenery as is afforded them in the Shetland Islands*'.

I do not think it was Shetland that narrowed down the spiritual vision of his later years.

I have tried for many years to track down Reid originals, to no avail. He is recorded as having exhibited watercolours many times at the Royal Scottish Academy. 'Two a penny, Victorian water-colourists!' was the comment from one uninterested art dealer.

For his book on the Highlands and Islands, Reid was based in the family home in Edinburgh and went on fortnightly forays to points North and West. Shetland is another country, a far country – even nowadays, despite air travel. He sketched and sojourned amongst the islands for the months of May and June of 1867–69.

*   *   *

May and June in Shetland. What better time for any artist with endless days of *simmer dim* . . .

> Here rise no groves, and here no gardens blow,
> Here even the hardy heath scarce dares to grow;
> But rocks on rocks, in mist and storm array'd,
> Stretch far to sea their giant colonnade.
> With many a cavern seam'd, the dreary haunt
> Of the dun seal and swarthy cormorant,
> Wild, round their rifted brows with frequent cry,
> As of lament, the gulls and gannets fly,
> And from their sable base, with sullen sound,
> In sheets of whitening foam the waves rebound.

Reid chose this poem by Sir Walter Scott for the title page of *Art Rambles in Shetland*. Like many Victorians, he was excited by Scott's bleak Gothic poetry and prose, and had read *The Pirate*, published in 1822, which was based on Scott's 1814 notes and diaries of his time in Shetland as a visiting Commissioner for Northern Lighthouses. The *Edinburgh Magazine*, reviewing the book, described Scott as a 'Delineator of Nature'. This would be dear to Reid's heart and in his own way, later in the century, he set out to do the same.

Reid was an illustrator, as well as a writer. That, and our distance in time, is my attraction to his work. For us both, words alone are sometimes inadequate in 'delineating Nature'.

We leave that to our chosen poets. The poem I have chosen is by Christine de Luca.

Wasterwick

Wasterwick, auld wife o da sea, worn
tae a beauty only age can bring. Du sits
straight-backed, airms reck oot
bi clett and stack. Dy sang is
da sang o sels an a thoosand shiftin shalls
is dey beach demsels. Da Waarie Gyo
is a secret fowld id y skurt, whaar
a kittle o tang swills to and fro.

Du gies houseroom tae a swap o scarfs
lodgins ta mallies. A shjalder swanks
apö dy shooder, nest safe in a reffel
o trefoil an smora. Banks-flooers
mak a wavy aedge ta dy simmer hap.

We look on dee at's cradled grown men,
Trace lines o kennin on dy wise repose.
Da wasterin sun at faas saaftly lays
A wild rose apo dy granite face.

shalls shells; *gyo* steep, narrow inlet; *kittle* tickle; *scarfs* shags;
mallies fulmars; *shjalder* oystercatcher; *smora* clover; *banks-flooers*
sea pinks; *hap* shawl

Mairi Hedderwick,
ISLE OF COLL,
12 April 2011

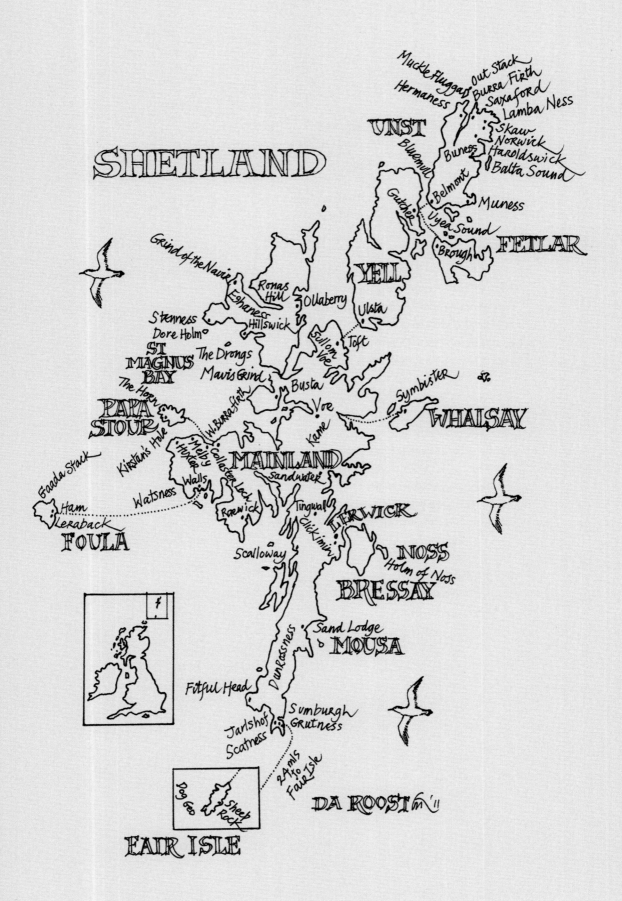

CHAPTER I

A Lengthy Introduction to Lerwick

JTR *A few days after the wreck of the Shetland mailsteamer,* Prince Consort, *in May 1867, I sailed from Leith for Lerwick on board the schooner* Matchless *'a splendid clipper' now in hale old age, yet of so graceful a build, and kept so trig and tidy, that she looked more youthful than many a younger sister that had seen fewer winters and sailed over calmer seas.*

Such a nonchalant introduction to a book and a sea journey.

The *Prince Consort*, belonging to the Leith and Clyde Shipping Co., struck rocks three miles south of Aberdeen in dense fog. There were 50 passengers and 33 crew on board. All were saved, despite one of the ship's lifeboats being swamped. Local salmon fishermen helped to get everyone ashore. The skipper, Captain Parrot, stayed on board until only the funnel showed above water.

Many passengers lost all their possessions and money. In a short time, the beach was covered with bedding, bonnets and clothing, chests of spirits, sugar and tea, sacks of doughy flour and bales of cloth. A Shetlander returning home from Australia lost all his hard won riches.

The shipping company provided accommodation and transport but many walked home the three wet miles to Aberdeen.

Captain Parrot was reprimanded at the official inquiry on 11 June but 'at the same time the Court would not be doing justice to the matter . . . if it did not say that his conduct prior to, and subsequent to the disaster, was in the highest degree creditable to him'.

To the relief of Captain Parrot, the *Prince Consort* was heavily insured.

Although sea travel in Reid's time was dangerous and unpredictable, no matter whether by steam or sail, it was the most common mode of transport and safer than coaching, where wheels regularly fell off and land pirates waited in remote areas. The new railways had comfortably opened up locations that could previously have only been reached by boat. However, there was only one way to get to Shetland.

I could not replicate Reid's nautical adventure, given time constraints and my unpredictable stability in small boats. I could have flown from Inverness or Aberdeen, which I have done many times, but that would have been cheating and, anyway, I planned to take my elderly Land Rover, kitted out with sleeping platform in the back and kettle for plugging into the cigarette lighter in the front. Going on the 12-hour overnight boat from Aberdeen to Lerwick would be a novelty, and authentic, being the contemporary means of public sea transport to Shetland.

It took Reid five days to get from Leith to Lerwick. The *Matchless* was becalmed off Arbroath for a day, giving passengers time to muse on their proximity to the 'Fairport' of Scott's *Antiquary*, which led to '*thoughts by an easy transition to the kindred story of "The Pirate", the tale which has its scene laid in the islands for which we were bound*'.

*   *   *

Scott, truly, was the first tourist officer for Scotland – and Shetland. Reid carried on the baton. Their books were not specifically travel books, as such. Those were coming off the presses in great quantities in response to the general public's new-found ability to travel for travel's sake. The Trossachs crawled with 'excursionists' out for the day from Glasgow and Edinburgh. It would take until the middle of the twentieth century before tourism of any significance became an industry in Shetland. That water in between.

Reid wanted to '*contribute something to the interest in these Islands which has been recently awakening here in the South . . .*' He was passionate to share with the reader his undoubted exultation in the wildness and grandeur of the landscape. '*Intelligent admirers of the beautiful in Nature do not confine their interest to one type of beauty: the stern has its attractions for them as well as the sweet.*'

Whilst sketching in the Trossachs and Arran, Reid was one of many tourists and Brother Brushes, his name for other travelling artists. He met no tourists or artists in Shetland. Maybe that is another reason why I prefer his Shetland book. It could have been 1867 when I was following many of his routes on the Mainland, as much as on the outlying islands. Days went by without seeing another human being.

*　　*　　*

It took me 15 days to get to Lerwick from the Isle of Coll in the Inner Hebrides.

After months of planning and studying the five Ordnance Survey (OS) maps that cover the twelve islands that Reid visited, reading and rereading the very rare copy of his book that Shetland antiquarian book dealers Janet Smith and Margaret and Robert Johnson helped to track down, the dawn of the expedition was Hebridean blue when I left home. A clear skied omen for my journey to the Land of the Midnight Sun.

I had decided to take the kitted-out Land Rover because there were no hostelries in Shetland of the kind that Reid and I had been able to share in the Highlands. Except for Lerwick, where *an enterprising hotel-keeper rented a block of buildings fronting the sea, and opened a commodious hotel, which is a great boon to tourists and travellers*. Everywhere else it was customary for Reid and those of his class to be given hospitality in the landowner's *Haa*, or the home of the minister or teacher.

Two months of B&Bs would have depressed me and my purse. And those contacts I did have on Shetland I shamefully avoided telling of my ploy. It was only Reid who knew where I went each day. Having travelling privacy, I could seek out hidden places. The maps promised many wilderness tracks for the end of each day. I would indulge in a hotel every four or five days for the purpose of cleanliness and society. And, as it turned out, by pleasant necessity, lodge with families on Foula and Fair Isle.

*　　*　　*

There had been an irritating, slipping reverse gear in the Land Rover, but that was to be sorted in Inverness en route for Aberdeen. The mechanic knew the whys and wherefores of my journey. 'You'll just not have to use reverse and you'll be fine,' his cheery comment. 'Otherwise it will have to be a reconditioned gearbox. Take a couple of days to track one down.'

I chose Otherwise.

Many 'couple of days' passed. There was no point going back home. A house-sitter friend had long looked forward to his holiday on Coll. I would not have been good company if I had returned.

With a heavy heart and heavier rucksack, I set off by train to Aberdeen to catch the 7 p.m. overnight sailing to Shetland. The rucksack was packed with maps and essentials, and photocopies of the pages of *Art Rambles in Shetland* stuffed down one of its pockets. The one and only concession to modernity, a mobile phone, stuffed down the other. The mechanic would let me know when to come back to collect the Land Rover. 'Could be a week or more . . .'

At North Link's pier office, I learned that there were no berths available on MV *Hrossey*. 'It's that ash from Iceland,' the clerk explained. He offered the last recliner. Thankfully not in the middle block, as in an aircraft, but to the side and facing a wall. The floor looked comfortable.

*   *   *

MV *Hrossey* is the sister ship to MV *Hjaltland*. Their names are the Old Norse for Orkney and Shetland. They ply the waters between mainland Scotland, Orkney and Shetland where Reid's '*German Sea*' meets the Atlantic and all that that encounter entails.

The tidal race of the *roost* streams between Sumburgh Head and Fair Isle. The demons of the deep await. How sensible to have overnight sailings. But that is not the reason. Shetlanders have long fought to retain the nightly service, as business, shopping and more can be achieved in a day in Aberdeen and the return overnight journey slept away.

Oh! for that service from CalMac in the Hebrides!

These car ferries are mini cruise ships. Bars, shops, cafeterias, a silver service restaurant, a cinema and 365 en suite cabins. No swimming pools, but excellent showers even for us in the recliners.

MV *Hrossey* inched slowly along the narrow canal-like reach of the docks, leaving behind the grey tones of Aberdeen, enlivened by the red, white and yellow of oil supply ships fading under a thin sun.

The open sea fretted at the final breakwater; the engines thrummed in anticipation. We were on our way.

It was time to explore the wonderland within. The shipping forecast had indicated Force 3 to 4. I would have dinner aboard.

The low-lit Ladeberry Restaurant, glass-partitioned from the main drag of brightly lit bars and cafeterias, had white long draped tablecloths and black linen napkins. The service was decorous and formal. How it reminded me, but without carpets and full length curtains, of early MacBrayne journeys to the Hebrides. The steward with white folded napkin over his arm taking orders, steady feet well apart; the jingling cutlery and china in counterpoint to the thump of the engines and the thrash of the waves at the porthole.

The Ladeberry's trimmed cutlets of Shetland lamb heard not a knife or fork jingle or an engine thump.

I was feeling much better, walking boots neatly tucked under the tablecloth.

A late postprandial wander took me up to the windows on the top deck, overlooking the bow. To starboard, for'ard and port, the thin light of mainland Scotland hid low behind a pearly sky. All sight of land gone. Looking down at the flat calm of the sea stretching for ever ahead, the silent ship took on a ghostly quality. Like a skimming cipher leading us all on the sea road to the world's end.

*   *   *

Finding accommodation in Lerwick was not easy. The hotels were very pricey and would not consider a reduction for a week's stay. B&Bs were all full. Damn that gearbox.

At any time of year this is the case, I was told, with oil executives in the hotels and workers in the B&Bs. This summer of 2010 was also the *Hamefarin*, when thousands of Shetlanders from all over the world come back 'home'. Held every 25 years, it is a fortnight's celebration of music, dance and literature, talks and exhibitions, tours to the other islands and endless socialising with relatives.

The celebration of the *Hamefarin* affirms a sense of identity for residents and *hamefarers* alike. Tourists the *hamefarers* are definitely not. The atmosphere in Lerwick was that of one great family holiday outing that elbowed out the Italian cruise ship passengers and

EVENING VIEW OF LERWICK.

Swedish yachties weaving their bemused way along the narrow alleyway of Commercial St.

The new Museum and Archives at restored Hay's Dock recorded nearly 11,000 visitors during the event. For some of the *hamefarers* it is a once in a lifetime, once in a generation, event. They come predominately from Australia and New Zealand to where their forebears had emigrated, not always by choice, in the nineteenth century.

JTR *Lerwick has one main street running parallel with the edge of the water and on each side houses, shops and warehouses are built, with the utmost disregard of everything and everybody save the convenience of the individual proprietor. Thus one gentleman from his front window has for view his neighbour's gable; and some houses are planted in the centre of the street, rendering it in parts so narrow that two people can scarcely walk abreast with any degree of comfort. It is all paved with flag-stones, and numerous narrow by-lanes lead up to the carriage-road on the Hill-Head; while shaggy little shelties, with well balanced loads of peat, walk leisurely alongside of the foot-passengers, following women, who, while bearing a like burden, are ever busily engaged knit, knitting at what seems the never-ending stocking.*

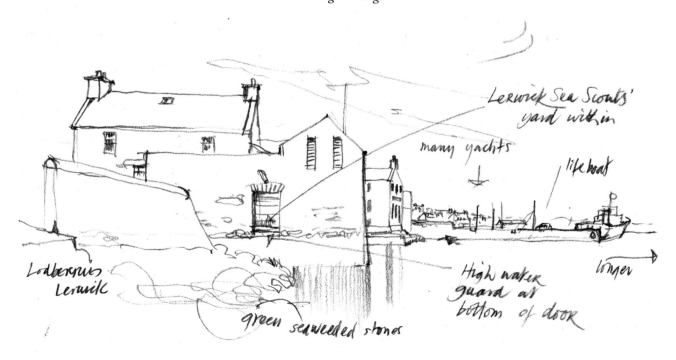

Lodberries .
LERWICK

The knitting women were part of the notorious Truck System of payment for goods or services. Money never left the merchant's purse. Instead they dictated the barter value of basic commodities in relation to the labourer's time or goods.

> Another day older and deeper in debt
> St Peter don't you call me 'cause I can't go
> I owe my soul to the company store.
> from work song 'Sixteen Tons'
by Tennessee Ernie Ford

All labouring classes were thralled to the system, landowners as controlling as merchants. Fishermen had to sell their catch to their landlord and were 'paid' in goods from the fish trader's own store.

In 1852, the Highland and Island Emigration Society was founded. By the time Reid arrived in Shetland, destitute thousands had already been given free passage to the colonies.

I wondered how many of the owners of Antipodean accents jostling with those of the Shetland dialect could have been direct descendants of Reid's knitting women, who had walked along the same well-worn flagstones.

The Shetland dialect is so distinctive, and definitely Scandinavian in lilt and emphasis. And regardless of its ancient origins is most modern; it is *the* language for texting. And there in the Spider's Web at the end of *Da Street* an enterprising Shetlander has knitted Fair Isle 'texting gloves' – without thumb and forefinger.

Reid '*found comfortable quarters at Mrs Slater's, next door to the post-office*' after rejecting the local boatman who had claimed him on the *Matchless* as she anchored in Bressay Sound. On sighting of a passenger boat, flotillas of little craft sculled furiously out from the shore and made fast to the hull. The boatmen '*jumped on board and rushed about in search of a* fare *in the shape of a passenger and his baggage: and, as a rule, the boatman who then takes you ashore considers he has a right to you during your stay in Lerwick*'.

The boatman's accommodation was not to Reid's liking. A tiny room had a two-storeyed box bed, the bottom half of which was already let. The exclusive use of the top half was not assured. The boatman '*hinted that a strange bedfellow might at times turn in along with me*'.

For myself, the Youth Hostel was full and the B&B I finally

PICTISH CASTLE—NEAR LERWICK.

found high up on Hillhead was thanks to a cancellation. 'But only for tonight,' said the matter-of-fact landlady. 'You'll not get anywhere. It's the *Hamefarin.*'

*   *   *

Public transport in Shetland is excellent. The Mainland is well served, with broad, sweeping roads all leading to and from Lerwick. Car ferries link all the islands save Foula and Fair Isle. A ridiculously small fare gives free access back and forth on the North Isles of Yell, Fetlar and Unst.

This I would learn once I got my wheels back. For the present, I

was carried onwards on the trail of Mr Reid by the bigger wheels of John Leask & Son.

JTR *About half a mile from Lerwick, in a valley, and close to the sea, is Clikamin, a small freshwater loch, in the centre of which are the ruins of one of the circular burghs so numerous in the Shetland Isles . . . In this loch, in summer, numbers of boys sail their miniature boats; here likewise the Baptists baptize their converts; and by its banks the Lerwegians are wont to have their larger washings, stamping their blankets, after the Scotch fashion, with their feet, and drying them over the drystane dykes.*

Three-thousand-year-old Clickimin Broch's remains are no longer near the sea. In that direction, spread over infill adjoining the main road, is Shetland's Tesco. Halfway round the loch is the red-roofed Clickimin Centre, one of the many magnificent leisure centres found throughout the Mainland and islands.

Boys can learn canoeing there, babies can have secular immersion in the toddlers' pool and washerwomen can choose from a multitude of cleaning powders and liquids in Tesco.

*   *   *

Despite free travel, courtesy of the Scottish Government and the Leasks, I was fretting at my lack of independent mobility. The urbanity of waiting in the Tesco bus stop, so near to such ancient history, was dispiriting. Listless Shetland ponies, grey with road dust, hung their heads over the fence. It was not Reid's Shetland – nor mine.

Clickimin Broch
LERWICK

CHAPTER II

A Bus to Scalloway, a Boat to Bressay and a One-way Bus Ticket to Sumburgh

JTR *From the hill above Scalloway an extensive and beautiful view can be had of the village, castle, and the islands to the westward; but owing to my bad fortune in being ever overtaken by the mists so prevalent in Shetland, I never saw it to advantage.*

I was the only passenger in the bus climbing the hill up out of Lerwick and into a sea fog at the top. Stone walls, heather and grassland moors with commercial peat fields sworled into the mist. By the time we got to the hill above Scalloway the fog had lifted and there was a fleeting glimpse of Reid's view, as the bus swung round the high alpine corner at an alarming rate and descended the steep slope below a massive quarry that was soon to be closed to re-route the hairpin bend we had just flown around.

The bus stop was at sea level. There was nothing for it but to climb back up the steep slope to that viewpoint corner. To go back up by the road was obviously dangerous. I took a path through small workshop units. Individual blue, purple and red Scandinavian-style wooden houses stretched along the shore. Halfway up the track, a large new house was poised, overlooking the view. I discreetly detoured. I thought I could see ruins on the precipitous incline below the corner barrier, possibly the foundations of the cottage in the foreground of Reid's engraving.

A fenced-in henhouse was near to the spot. Moving about to get the exact angle, I finally settled and sat by the fence to sketch. I was aware of a woman lingering at a window in the house below. Eventually she came out the door and climbed towards me. 'Just checking the hens have not got out . . .' she said, whilst looking enquiringly at the sketchbook.

Vaila, so named for the island far west of Scalloway, was relieved and fascinated by the old engraving. 'The foundations for our house must have come from that old ruin in the picture.'

SCALLOWAY.

It transpired that her husband had phoned from his workplace far below. 'There's someone wandering around about the henhouse . . .'

JTR *I spent a day sketching the old mill; and many a pilgrim from the peat hill halted at the bridge, resting for a few minutes their burdens to gaze inquisitively at what I was about. One old woman, at the sight of the old mill on paper, waxed eloquent as she recalled the memories of other years.*

In search of the old mill, I went back down the hill. As I passed the workshops there was no sign of anyone once more. I hoped Vaila had phoned her husband.

A man painting his fence on Mill Brae pointed to the stream that wound its way through a grassland strath towards the sea. It disappeared under the new road, sweeping over a three-tunnel concrete bridge to emerge on the other side, seaweed at its edges.

'Aye, that's the Mill Burn. There's nothing left of the Mill now,' he said. Its stones no doubt poached for the new road and bridge. In living memory, he said, when ice formed by the old bridge, the fishermen would collect great chunks of it for the boats.

Looking up the deserted valley, the only signs of comparable industry were the tops of giant white wind-turbine blades slicing the sky at the back of the Burra Dale ridge.

Scalloway was the ancient capital of Shetland. The ruin of Scalloway Castle, built by the infamous Earl Patrick Stewart in 1600, stands testimony to oppressive past times. The huddle of cottages snug below its walls in Reid's image is mostly gone. The sea used to be nearer to the castle. Infill has created an extensive car park and jetty jutting out into the bay. It was quite deserted.

Compared to the daily hustle and bustle of Lerwick *en Hamefarin fête,* Scalloway was like drifting on a gentle eddy in an ancient backwater.

Scalloway

COTTAGES NEAR SCALLOWAY.

In the tiny museum further along the main street, two elderly lady volunteers were keen to tell about the new museum that is being built adjoining the castle. Their lovingly jam-packed idiosyncratic displays would no doubt get a makeover, and a computer screen would show films of seabirds and sunsets.

The lady with a strong Shetland dialect did most of the talking; her friend, from mainland Scotland, or even mainland Britain, a *sooth moother*, itched to say she was not a local. 'Neither am I,' said the Shetlander, firmly. 'I am from Unst.'

On the seafront is the monument to The Shetland Bus. During World War II, Norwegians escaping from German-occupied Norway found safe harbour in Scalloway after coming across the North Sea in fleets of ostensibly working fishing boats. Traffic was

Vaila's
Hen house

Scalloway

two way, as British agents used the return passage to get into Norway. From 1941 to 1945, the 'buses' went back and forth. The monument is in the shape of a cairn, made up of stones from Shetland and Norway. Those from Norway came from the home district of the 44 sailors who gave their lives to the Resistance Movement. On top is a sculpture of the *Andhoven*, one of the 'bus' boats, riding the crest of a wave.

Walking along the opposite side of the quiet street comes a little boy, all of three or four years old, followed by a black lamb with a red collar. Taken aback, I smile. He smiles. And then a man runs along the street. 'You know you should not go out of the garden!' he shouts, swinging the child up into his arms. The boy buries his head on his father's shoulder in remorse. They turn back, the lamb following obediently without any telling, its tiny hooves click-clacking on the pavement. They go into a garden that fronts onto the road, the gate firmly shut behind them.

One day that lamb will be a big black sheep, red collar or no red collar.

*　　*　　*

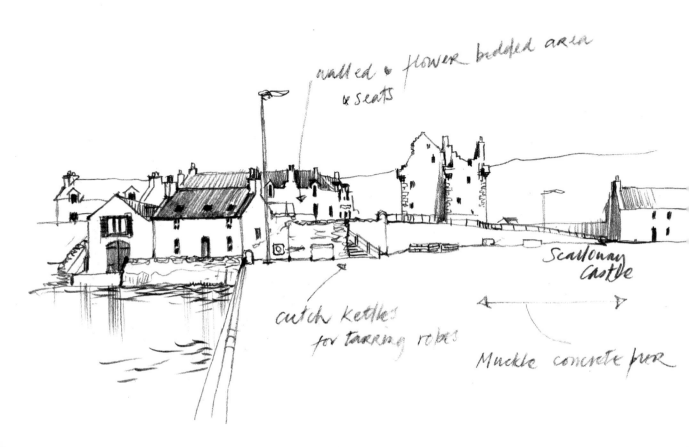

walled & flower bedded area & seats

cutch kettles for tarring ropes

Scalloway Castle

Muckle concrete pier

OLD MILL—SCALLOWAY.

SCALLOWAY CASTLE.

Reid observed lambs in Scalloway.

'. . . and the sheep, like Jacob's flock, are grotesquely spotted and marked, black, moorit, and white. The lambs are curious little creatures. I observed, with some amusement, a spotted ewe superintending the gambols of two frisking lambkins – one black with a white head and tail, the other white with black spectacles and a black nose.'

At the very end of the road that curves round the bay is the North Atlantic Fisheries College, part of the University of the Highlands and Islands. It is also the Centre for Nordic Studies and home to the best restaurant I had discovered in Shetland so far. Seafood top of the menu, of course. But before a fillet of Shetland salmon with crab crushed potatoes, the potted rabbit with home-made piccalilli was a tasty starter.

Da Haaf restaurant was the busiest place in Scalloway.

When I eventually got the Land Rover back, it was noticeable the number of times whilst on the mainland that I detoured back to Scalloway of an evening.

*　　*　　*

Back in Lerwick that night in yet another B&B, I knew I had to get away from streets and people and bus timetables and find the Shetland that I really had come to explore with Mr Reid.

Next morning I was on the Victoria pier waiting for the first ferry coming over from Bressay, the island on the other side of the Sound.

Commuters to the Mainland streamed off in packed vehicles and on foot. Secondary schoolchildren for the Anderson Institute in Lerwick humped heavy eyes and bags off the ramp. A white van man stalled and everyone shoved.

Further along the pier, the 1900 'Fifie' sailing ship *Swan* was moored, the twelve passengers still below decks oblivious to the chaos above. Hundreds of pier-nesting terns were screaming all round, disturbed by the commotion of the start to a Lerwick day.

Like the bus to Scalloway, I had MV *Lierna* practically to myself save for the taxi carrying the island's mail. Reid's purpose in going to Bressay was to cross over the island to the neighbouring island of Noss, where cliffs of nearly 600 feet rise from the sea. A Victorian artist's dream subject for sketching.

The local mail bus with seats for passengers was no more. Now

LERWICK.

the taxi delivered the mail, but not in a circular route, which meant I could get a non-return lift to the crossing for Noss. The three-and-a-half mile walk back for the last Bressay ferry to Lerwick meant an eye to the clock for my day away from civilisation.

Once again the morning had started with a *haar* that clung to the moor on the way over to Reid's ferryman's cottage opposite Noss.

JTR   *On reaching the ferryman's cottage, his wife informed me that he was out fishing; she signalled to the shepherd, who chanced to be tarring his boat on the opposite beach, to come for me, mentioning in commendation of that worthy, 'he's a Shetlander, and nane o' thae Scotch bodies!'* [Ah! I wonder if the need for that definition still obtains today!] *The Sound, though narrow, is often boisterous and quite impassable. With hearty vigour he ferried me across, and as I had a letter to him from his master, the enterprising Scotch farmer who rents the island for pasturing sheep, he and his wife left no stone unturned whereby they might minister to my comfort.*

*   *   *

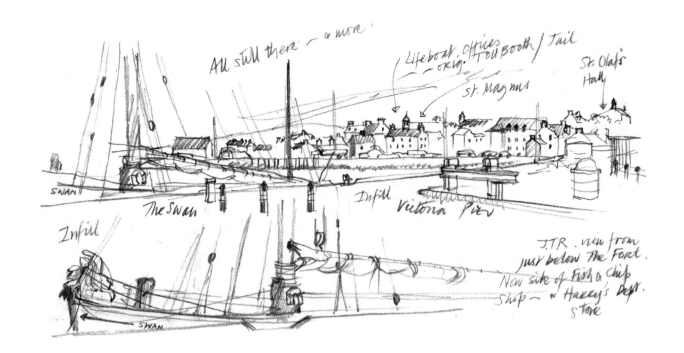

All still there ~ ~ more

Lifeboat. Offices Toll Booth / Jail
orig.

St. Magnus

St. Olaf's Hall

SWAN

The Swan

Infill

Victoria Pier

Infill

SWAN

J.T.R. view from
just below The Fort.
Now site of Fish & Chip
Shop ~ & Harry's Dept.
Store

Victoria Pier · Lerwick.

FERRYMAN'S COTTAGE, BRESSAY.

Since 793 Shetland had been a Norse colony. In 1468, Margaret, daughter of King Christian I of Denmark and Norway was engaged to James III of Scotland. Her dowry was never fully paid so her father pledged Shetland, in lieu, to Scotland in 1469, the year of the marriage. This was the beginning of an incursion of Scottish traders, entrepreneurs, missionaries and landowners, the latter being the agents for fundamental change in the ownership of land.

Shetland used the Norse *udal* form of land law which, similar in a way to the clan system in the Highlands and Islands, did not have the concept of 'ownership' of land. The land belonged to everyone, and in *udal* law the right to the seashore, especially, did not suit the new landowners. (This is still a contentious subject in Shetland.)

As Shetland trade and industries developed, culminating in the profitable years of the herring and kelp, whaling, sheep rearing and mineral extraction, large country mansions were built on every island with no expense spared, landowners vying with each other for

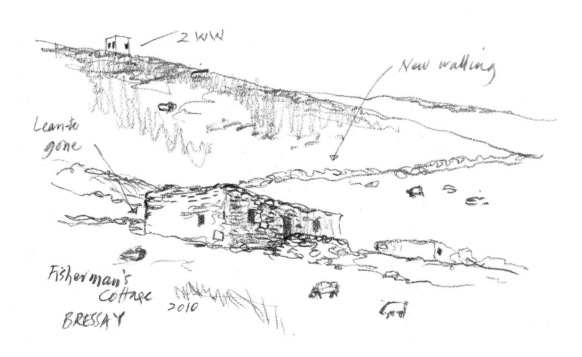

the latest style and fashion. Labour was cheap. The Truck System made sure that the islanders were trapped in grinding poverty and available for work. It would be into the 1870s before the system was addressed by a Commission of Enquiry to the discomfiture of many landowners.

Reid, as was his privilege, would have rested his head under the grandiose roofs when travelling in the vicinity. Was he ignorant of the oppressive conditions controlled by his hosts? He certainly makes no political comment in either of his books.

His hosts were for the most part of Scots or English extraction. The ferryman's wife's memory was very long.

*   *   *

I, too, had to wait for a crossing. A sign said 'Boat at 10 am'.

The ferryman's house is still standing on the slope of the hill leading down to the water's edge. Roofless, the sheep graze in amongst the fallen stones. On Noss, a deceptive stone's throw away over the water, is the shepherd's house on a green sward promontory, a curved beach of cream sand at its back. It has a roof and a radio mast. There the island warden lives; the only inhabitant of Noss, all of 774 acres. Scottish Natural Heritage manage the island as a nature reserve by agreement with the owner, who works it as a sheep farm.

With a flourish of the outboard motor mid channel to counteract the current, over comes the inflatable with two crofters aboard. They had already completed shepherding duties for the owner. The stylish steersman is Alex, the steerswoman warden.

To walk the coastline of Noss with time to stand and stare takes about four hours. The boots and the little rucksack '*well charged with stores for the soul, the mind, the brush, and the body . . .*' were ready to go. The ghostly sheer-drop headlands of the Ward of Bressay stretched to the southwest, a freshening wind nudging the waves towards the island, as the sun sieved through the thinning fog. It promised to be a blue-skied day. Close to the rocky shore the old schooner *Swan,* in full hopeful sail, slowly glided eastwards towards the Holm and the Noup of Noss.

The coastal path wound onwards and upwards, seabirds weaving on thermals above my head. Not a human in sight. This was the Shetland I wanted.

Reid mentions passing several ruins of fishermen's cottages as he

THE CRADLE OF NOSS.

heads for the '*far-famed "Holm of Noss"*'. Did he make any connection between them and the '*enterprising Scotch farmer*'? The ruins are now part of an impressive dyke, crumbling in places, that encircles Noss with distinctive thin, almost slate-like upright copings.

A holm is an ample islet that rises considerably from the sea but is not narrow like a stack. At the southerly point of Noss, there is such a feature, all of 180 feet high and with good grazing on top. Now commonly known as the Cradle of Noss on account of a Bressay man who, promised the reward of a cow, created a box cradle with room enough for a man and a sheep to cross from Noss

ex·
Cradle
of Noss

orange lichen tops
of copings

to the Holm by means of ropes attached at the top of the opposing cliffs. Thus many sheep were able to have good grazing and seabird eggs were easier to collect in the Spring.

Unfortunately, the man, having achieved the amazing feat of climbing first one cliff face and then the other to embed the stakes for attaching the ropes, decided on his return not to use the novel access made by himself and, in starting to climb back down the cliff, fell to his death.

This happened 200 years previous to Reid's visit, according to the shepherd who accompanied him. Reid's engraving shows the cradle still in use.

The Cradle of Noss
& the Swan

JTR *In connection with the cradle, I heard of a singular mishap which befell a person who crossed to the holm by means of it, packed it with a choice collection of young scories, and got in on the top of them to make the return journey. Unfortunately, when half-way over the fearful abyss, the bottom of the cradle gave way, the poor young gulls, not yet able to fly, went down like a shot, and the gentleman, clinging tenaciously to its sides, reached the opposite bank in rather a nervous condition.*

There is no sign of the ingenious contraption nowadays. The gap between the two precipitous edges made a dramatic frame for the *Swan* far below, instead.

The path rose to an abrupt cliff edge, where suddenly, stunningly, the whole of the Noup was in view. One hundred and eighty feet of startling guano-whitened rock thrust up from the sea; thousands of gannets nesting, wheeling back and forth and diving deep below me. Inches over the edge puffins looked up with

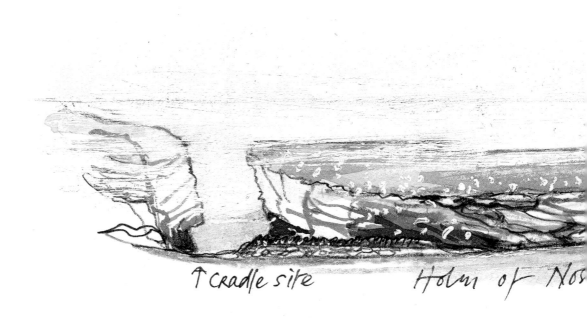

↑ cradle site   Holm of Nos

clownish interest in between jostling cackling fulmars off their precipitous patch.

JTR   *Strange sight! To gaze from such a vantage-point and see the untold myriads of the tribes of the air floating 'tween sky and sea, even as a snow-shower in a wintry day.*

Reid would not have seen any gannets; it was not until 1914 that gannets, following the changing movements of fish, first bred on the Noup.

Looking backwards, I could see later human arrivals making their way up the incline. Instinctively I wanted to move quickly on but snuck in against the dyke just to see the reaction on their faces as they crested the rise and saw the Noup. It was worth the wait.

The warden's cottage was deserted when I got back for the crossing to Bressay. A note with a marked map on the door said, 'Just gone to Papil Hill to look for Orcas – seen by a boat.' A

- waiting for the haar to lift as usual .

THE NOUP OF NOSS.

camera-festooned couple dashed off – ran, actually – over the moor to the north, in the direction indicated. What is the whale equivalent of a twitcher? A finner? I cannot understand this obsession with sightings of whales. Will they not exist if they are not *seen*? A kind of validation, similar to 'I saw it in the papers . . .', 'I saw its fin above the water . . .'

The extremely low roofed steadings at the back of the cottage intrigued me. An information board told the story of the Pony Pund. In 1871, the Marquis of Londonderry set up a stud farm on Bressay and Noss to breed Shetland ponies for haulage in his coal mines in Durham. He had a long-term project in mind, the 1842 ban on child labour his motivation. He selected six foundation Shetland stallions and with careful breeding produced the miniature Shetland; 'strong and weighty in body, legs as near the ground as possible'.

I always thought miniature Shetlands were created for doting Victorian Papas and Mamas, for their befrilled and beribboned offspring to pose upon in front of sepia-tinted mansions. I have an image of the Marquis and his family above ground posing for such a photograph and deep down below the lawn and rose beds the crawling coal-blacked children of Durham.

No, it was hard capitalist cash that produced the breed.

Wandering and wondering in the Pony Pund passed pleasant time till Alex and the 'finners' came back, breathless.

I had missed out on the possible drama of the Orcas attacking and devouring seals that favoured a particular platform of rock 100 feet below Papil Hill. As it turned out, the Orcas had glided on and out to sea, just leaving their fins to photograph.

*   *   *

It was late evening by the time I got to the Bressay ferry after my first wild day on Shetland. The lights of Lerwick over the water made me muse on my eternal dilemma: which is better, if one had to make the choice, to live in the wilds and look over to urban sprawl or to live in a town and look over to wilderness?

Reid would have had difficulty seeing Lerwick as his Bressay ferryman steered past the fretwork of hundreds of masts belonging to the fleet of Dutch *busses* moored in the Sound at this similar time of year. These two- or three-masted fishing vessels followed the herring and were big enough to *gib*, or salt fish, on board and so travel great distances from the Netherlands. The much anticipated arrival of the fleet at the end of June was an important time of trade for Shetlanders and coincided with the local celebration of Johnsmas.

Pony races and wagers were held for the amusement of the Dutch crews whose wooden-shod feet touched the ground on either side of the diminutive mounts. The amusement of the Lerwegians was to poke the rear of the ponies as they left the starting line, count the fallen, inebriated Dutch and collect easy money.

JTR   *Towards the end of June is Johnsmas, an important day in the Shetland calendar. For centuries past it has been the custom for the fleet of Dutch fishing 'busses' to frequent Bressay Sound at that time.*

Reid describes the unusual sight, for him, of '*these strange and antiquated-looking crafts, with their highly polished oak sides, gaily painted bulwarks, and many-coloured flags*'.

* * *

I had been spoilt by my day on Noss. I wanted wide open spaces on another small island. No *hamefarers,* no researching in the Shetland Archives or the Tourist Office, no dodging the serious man handing out leaflets at the 'Shetland for Independence from Scotland' stall bedecked with Shetland flags on Commercial Street. He had my total sympathy and understanding, but oh! for escape to the sea and cliffs again.

* * *

Early next day I was at the bus station, getting a one-way ticket to Sumburgh en route for the boat to Fair Isle.

FAIR ISLE FROM SUMBURGH.

CHAPTER III

Escape to Fair Isle

Fair Isle lies southwest of Sumburgh Head and is roughly 25 miles equidistant between Shetland and North Ronaldsay, Orkney. The tidal vagary of notorious fame, *Da Roost*, is between Sumburgh and Fair Isle. The *Good Shepherd IV*, taking cargo and twelve passengers maximum, sails three times a week in summer and once a week in winter. The crossing is only about two and a half hours, *weather permitting*. Except in fair weather, the *Good Shepherd* is pulled up the slipway in the harbour of North Haven in Fair Isle after offloading passengers and supplies. Just in case.

A visit to the island, therefore, has to be planned well in advance, with a weather eye open and a philosophical turn of mind. There is a 25-minute flight from mainland Shetland which is often more reliable, as long as there is no sea fog. Either way of travel, accommodation has to be booked in advance. In the height of the season, weather *unpermitting*, however, a booked bed can only be assured if the previous occupant is not storm or fogbound on the

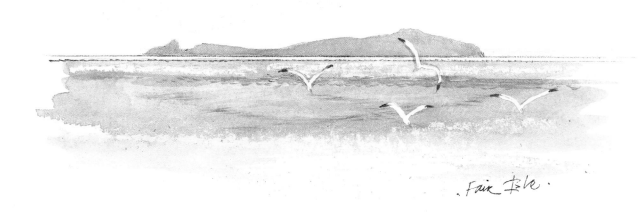

Fair Isle.

island. Therefore both parties are stranded. The mainlander, however, has room for manoeuvre.

In the interests of accurately following Reid, whenever I could, I walked from the bus to Grutness pier for the ten-thirty morning sailing to Fair Isle. The daily early-morning fog had lifted and warm sun promised an easy crossing.

On Grutness pier the *Good Shepherd* was unloading skips of metal rubbish, rusted white goods and punctured fishing floats from Fair Isle. It was the time of year for the *Clear Da Voes* Campaign. The derrick then swung over to lift and lower gas cylinders, diesel barrels, numerous crates, the suitcases of an elderly couple visiting friends on Fair Isle and my rucksack into the hold amidship. A sizeable caravan was then swung high and gently manoeuvred on to the top of the now covered hold. Its TV aerial caused one of the crew concern as it snagged on a sling and snapped off. 'Well,' said the other crew. '*Nae faat.* There's nae digital on Fair Isle.'

Neil, the skipper, said there was talk of a RoRo car ferry coming soon. I could not quite make out if this was a good thing or not.

By eleven-thirty, we were edging away from the pier and heading out of Grutness Voe.

There was a choice of seating; on the small, open deck space behind the wheelhouse or down the steep companionway below the wheelhouse to the saloon. 'Strap yourself into a seat, if you go down there,' advised the skipper. Myself and the elderly couple opted for the invigoration of the open deck and the sturdiness of the rails.

JTR *After a succession of gales, which detained me two weeks in Sumburgh, waiting for a favourable opportunity to make a passage to Fair Isle, succeeded a day of perfect calm. About six in the afternoon, a pleasant breeze sprung up, and we sailed from the little harbour of Grutness, hoping to reach Fair Isle by daylight next morning . . . Soon, however, a bank of cloud rose above the horizon . . . In a few minutes more, gusts of wind, gaining in force as they became more frequent, crested the billows as they rose with fringe of foam. Our skipper, expecting the wind to increase to a gale, knew that it would be impossible to make Fair Isle with so dense a mist, and foresaw that his only safety lay in finding his way back to Sumburgh.*

Three nights after, the weather enabled us to make a second start.

North Side
of Sheep Rock
Fair Isle

Being close to the wheelhouse, there was opportunity for *craic*. I
learned that the island had about 60 of a population, half locals and
half *sooth moothers*; the school expanding, the two churches lively
and that the major improvements to the Fair Isle Bird Observatory
were still not finished. 'There has been a lot of cargo recently,' said
the skipper.

I ask the question that is always foremost in my mind when
visiting small islands. Who owns the island? Land ownership of such
an islanded space crucially determines the definition of its society.

Since 1954 the whole of Fair Isle has belonged to the National
Trust. A good thing, say some, as all properties are fairly rented and
young people can afford to live on Fair Isle but, say others, they can
never get onto the property ladder.

I hear the romantic story of the previous owner, a young
ornithologist, who fell in love with Fair Isle whilst visiting in 1935.
George Waterston belonged to that class and time of adventurers
who sought out islands and isolated places to fulfil personal
ambitions and become part of remote community living. A little bit
of paternalism and private money was involved.

George wanted to build a bird observatory and develop and
market the unique Fair Isle knitting. World War II put paid to his
plans. But time spent in a German POW camp was not wasted. Fair
Isle and all that he intended to do for the island preoccupied him

SHEEP CRAIG, FAIR ISLE.

despite ill health. He was repatriated from the Baltic at the end of the war on a Swedish hospital ship. Crossing the North Sea, his first sighting of home land, in more ways than one, was the distinctive shape of Sheep Rock – or Sheep 'Craig', as Reid calls it – on the east coast of Fair Isle. George took that as a sign.

In 1947, he and his brother bought the island from Sumburgh Estates for the sum of £4,000. The vision that George had had since his youth became the blueprint for the island that it is today. He built the original Fair Isle Bird Observatory and tirelessly set up displays in city stores of Fair Isle knitting surrounded by photos of the island and its customs.

But ill health dogged him. In 1954, he sold Fair Isle to the National Trust for the same price that he had paid for it.

*   *   *

Sheep Rock & the Haar
Fair Isle

Reid was welcomed on Fair Isle by a bevy of young girls who had stood long on the cliff watching his boat take three hours to battle the morning tide before coming in to the harbour. The returning minister's housekeeper was really the focus of their excited attention after she and Reid had been ferried in a dinghy to '*slippery boulders, and carried on the back of one of the islanders to the shore*'. Whilst Reid '*not having the clerical white cravat, was set down as a much-dreaded and daily expected official, known all over Shetland, and even on this remote isle, as the "Dog-tax man"*'.

My hosts were waiting for me on the solidly built pier. As was the owner of the caravan. Accommodation on the island was at a premium because the unfinished Bird Observatory still housed workmen at the peak of the birdwatchers' year. The enterprising islander had hired the caravan for letting during these two critical tourist months.

Bill and Margo first came to Fair Isle in the mid '70s. They had previously toured in the Hebrides looking for that perfect haven and, unbeknownst to me, or, more accurately, completely forgotten by me (those were the chaotic young and extended family years of romantic self-sufficiency), had visited us on Coll. We became the exemplar of all they wanted to achieve, they told me, as we sat in the kitchen of their house overlooking black skerries stitched onto a silvered sea stretching to infinity.

They noted a National Trust advertisement for crofting tenants on Fair Isle and the rest was history. It was good to share the memories of what it was really like to live on remote islands in those days and what hard but rewarding work it was. But for all the modern communication links and services now provided to both islands, Coll's present day 'isolation' is a euphemism compared to that of Fair Isle. Foula even more so, as I was to find out.

Their original crofthouse over the field was mine. Freedom to walk all and every day, call in at the well-provisioned shop for supplies and return to Springfield to light the fire, read, study maps and take notes. 'But remember there is no electricity between 11.30 pm and 7.30 am. The diesel generator is shut down. Have you a torch?'

In 1962, with great publicity, the first commercially operated 60 kW wind turbine was installed on Fair Isle. It was community owned and funds were raised for a second of 100 kW to be built in 1996. The electricity generated supplemented the already existing diesel supply.

'The windmills are caput. We're waiting for parts that will never come. The windmills are too old,' said one disgruntled islander. And they surely were, all rusty and inactive in the ever whistling salt-laden wind. The island fuel bills have rocketed up, as more diesel has had to be used.

For myself, the still of the night was welcome without the throb of a generator. There was no need of a torch. The North Ronaldsay lighthouse on Orkney beamed into the bedroom with rhythmic illumination.

When the Orcadians sighted Viking ships, fire signals were sent from North Ronaldsay to Fair Isle and the message passed on from Ward Hill to the Mainland of Shetland. I slept easy in the sweeping axis of the past.

*   *   *

The days, as so often, started with seeping sea fog or *haar* coating the fields with dew. An early attempt to capture Reid's view of Sheep 'Craig' meant sitting for an hour or more mesmerised by the ever wreathing veils of mist. A tense pose; the steep, grassy slope slid easily down to the heaving, gasping and sucking waves. Eiders sashayed with the surges; ducks quacking, drakes coo-cooing like city pigeons in love. Fulmars cackled and squabbled. From the gannetry on Sheep Rock the gannets sounding harsh and angry, almost with lion- or hyena-like roars. No doubt doubly asserting their tenancy rights, as in Noss. In 1969, there were only three adults nesting on Fair Isle. By '73, there were 100 birds; in 2002, there was an estimated 1,585.

And yet despite the cacophony all else was eerily silent, save for the slap and slide of the dark grey waves below.

Fifty feet above there would be blue skies and a brassy sun.

Opposite on the dim headland inland from Sheep Rock I could make out Skeldie Kliv, the site of the nineteenth-century wreck of the *Lessing*.

JTR *A few weeks before I visited Fair Isle, the Lessing, a new ship on her first passage, was wrecked at Skeldie Cliff. She had only left Bremen a week before she struck, and was bound for New York, with a very miscellaneous cargo, and a hopeful band of emigrants from many European nationalities, one hundred and fifty of whom were women and children.*

Hol o'Klaver
& Klaver's Geo

Fair

In full sail at seven knots the *Lessing*, thinking she was 50 miles past Fair Isle, struck the cliff face with full force and was jammed into a narrow cleft. Lowered lifeboats were '*smashed to atoms*'.

'*We need not wonder that one loud, spontaneous yell of agony broke forth as the emigrants gazed around – a woeful cry, re-echoed by the screams of the sea-fowl that tenanted the rocks, and rousing the lonely islanders, who, while they could see nothing of the ship because of the density of the mist, yet, above the thunder of the breakers and the cry of the sea-birds, heard again and again the wild shriek of human woe. Finding out their position thus, they promptly hastened to their*

Sheep Rock

assistance through a remarkable tunnel called "Skeldie Cave".

Everyone was taken back through the cave to the base of 300-foot inland cliffs '*at the top of which stood all the women of the island in earnest consultation; as there was scarcely any meal on the island at the time, gloomy pictures of famine filled their troubled mind. But soon sympathy for the shipwrecked ones overcame every other consideration; and one by one they descended the steep path to help up their unfortunate sisters, carrying their children for them, and welcoming them to the shelter of their humble cottages, and a share of such fare as they possessed. Every cottage on the island was crowded, and the two little churches and a schoolroom were turned into temporary dormitories.'*

In 1868, the islanders received bravery awards and compensation from the German government. The male islanders, that is. One feisty woman and her daughter fought for recompense for the womenfolk of Fair Isle, their argument being that so many of them were sea widows and the only source of income for their families. It took a long time but perseverance won their case.

Islanders were always keen to correct Reid's spelling and place names. The *Lessing* struck Klaver's Geo; the tunnel is Hol o'Klaver. The OS is no more accurate; it cites Geo Claver. This is common, especially in remote places, as local names have been in intimate use for generations with little change, as incoming influences were few and far between. Coastline names came from the land being observed from the sea. The local fishermen 'fixed' the fishing grounds in relation to two or three recognisable landmarks. The names could refer to shape, historical and personal reference, tidal fluke and a host of other identifications essential to safe navigation.

There was one map reference on Fair Isle that could only be named from the land. It is not on the OS but on an old map belonging to my hosts. It is the Dog Geo, marked on the southwest coast between Mathers Head and Malcolm's Head.

Reid was discomfited at being taken for the '*Dog-tax man*'. He went on to reassure the islanders that he had '*no desire that the memory of my visit should serve as a tombstone to mark the time when many aged, infirm and ill-favoured members of the canine race departed this life in a precipitate manner by being thrown over the cliffs nearest their respective homes; for such, I believe, is the doom awaiting them when that gentleman shall arrive*'.

In the year and very month of Reid's visit to Fair Isle, *The Orcadian* carried this article:

> During last month about two-thirds of the dogs usually kept in Shetland were put to death, and yet more licences have been taken out here than perhaps any county in Scotland. Those tenants living near the hill pasture are obliged to keep dogs, ere they would not save their crops. There has been a great deal of grumbling about the licences, and many are afraid that they will have to pay for their pigs and hens. Loyal as the Shetlanders are, they abhor taxes in every name and form.

How many other political corrections of maps have removed markers of local history, unpleasant though this one certainly was?

*   *   *

Anne Sinclair is rightly proud of the museum she and her co-volunteers have created in the *Auld Skul*. Properly named The George Waterston Memorial Centre, it has a wealth of photos and memorabilia that only isolated communities can bring forth from cupboards and sheds safe from predating passers-by. There were many domestic items such as moulded glass-stemmed bowls and white gold-edged cream jugs that came from the 'floating shops' that anchored off the islands. 'American clocks', with North American carved surrounds, brought home or sent back by emigrants were as ubiquitous here as in the Hebrides. China doll heads from the *Lessing* waited for cloth body parts to be re-stitched on. Photographs of oxen in lieu of ponies that were used for field work until the 1950s. A mediaeval image.

And, of course, exquisite examples of Fair Isle knitting. I won't go into the issue of Shetland versus Fair Isle knitting patterns here. Suffice it to say that the generic label of 'Fair Isle' has been adopted by Shetland knitters and the specific is in danger of being lost.

*   *   *

Sun shone all day for the arrival of *The Spirit of Adventure* cruise ship. She and other cruise ships anchor off Fair Isle during the season and, in a reverse of the 'floating shops', passengers are ferried by rib to the island. The Village Hall is decorated and tables set out with islanders' work for sale. Long winter nights produce a wide range of knitting, crafts, photography, paintings, designer puffin hats and much more. There is a lot of creative talent on Fair Isle. But pride of place is devoted to tables of home-made cakes, biscuits and sponges oozing cream and jam. Mounds of neatly cut sandwiches surrounded urns hissing in anticipation of the influx of visitors.

It was unbelievable. The Captain of *The Spirit of Adventure* radioed to say that the swell was too big for the ribs to land. For islanders so in tune with the sea around them, there had been no doubt that the welcome visitors could not come ashore. 'Health and Safety' muttered someone.

The atmosphere of utter dejection and demoralisation as islanders packed up their belongings and cleared the tables was quite distressing. 'It's happened before. We're used to it,' said a lady putting her biscuits back in the tin. Disappointment turned to positive banter. 'Well, the bairns will have a good tea tonight!'

I bought as many books, cards and Fair Isle badges – oh! and a puffin hat – as the rucksack could hold. My final meal on Fair Isle was a plateful of meringues and éclairs and the eggiest of egg sandwiches. Not possibly the best of ballast for the next day's return to the Mainland on *Good Shepherd IV.*

Maybe the captain of the cruise ship had been right. A storm had been brewing. It was time to be strapped onto the bench seat in the saloon of the *Good Shepherd.* I was the only passenger and dignity was of no consequence. I did not strap myself in to one of the seats, for that meant sitting up. Lying down on a bench against the bulkhead, I wedged myself between it and the seats in front. Horizontal is my best defence against *mal de mer.* To describe the condition in French is less matter of fact and more mellifluous.

What a battering that boat and I took. At one point I saw, out of the corner of a teary eye, a member of the crew come down the companionway to see if I was alive. I stayed dead.

Never was a harbour more havenly as Grutness. I staggered off and headed for the stately pile of Sumburgh Hotel, ex-Sumburgh House, where the young laird had given hospitality to Reid. I did not care what it cost.

There were no rooms.

If I came back at five, there might be a cancellation. A French executive had not signed in yet. They were everywhere, those executives. I worked out I had two choices: bus to Lerwick or hang around with hope eternal. And then came the inspiration. I could see Sumburgh airport in the distance. Airports. Car hire. And thus it was I knew I would have a bed for the night and could stay in the area to get on with stalking Reid and be able to move around in my own time.

Parking Kia at the hotel to collect the rucksack, I just had to ask if the executive had arrived. No. Car or no Kia. I succumbed. I was not quite ready to sleep in a box on four wheels yet. I needed to kit her out.

CHAPTER IV

The Shortest Chapter

JTR *It was my good fortune before leaving Shetland to make the acquaintance of the young Laird of Sumburgh. I spent several weeks under his hospitable roof, and had opportunity of becoming familiar with that portion of the Shetland mainland . . . In 'The Pirate' Sir Walter pictures the scene below the bold promontory of Sumburgh Head as that of the wreck of Cleveland's disabled ship.*

Sir Walter also set part of his seventeenth-century novel in the old *Haa* of Sumburgh, which by the time of his arrival was a ruin. But he renamed it and gave it new life with a Scandinavian title, Jarlshof, meaning Earl's Mansion. Sir Walter, who died in 1832, would never have seen the extensive Viking site – and earlier ruins dating back 3,000 years – that first became exposed in storms in 1890. Nor would Reid.

JTR *The ruined walls of Jarlshoff still weather the blast; and, not many yards distant has risen, within the last two years, a stately pile of masonry, the fine new house of Sumburgh, which will, I doubt not, prove a most charming residence, thus romantically situated between Fitful, or the White Mountain, and Sumburgh, with a look-out over the ever-changeful* roost, *and a distant view of Fair Isle.*

I wonder what Reid and his laird host, Bruce of Sumburgh, would think of the '*romantic situation*' of Sumburgh House, with the roar and racket of the airport nearby, helicopters clattering back and forth over the immaculately lawned excavations of the Viking settlement. And the ugly two-storey flat-roofed extension to the '*stately pile of masonry*'; the eventual walled gardens and greenhouses that grow grapes no more, characterless rows of chalets in their place. Oil has brought many good things to Shetland but sadly not

RUINS OF JARLSHOFF.

this. Of all the places I travelled on the islands this site and sight were changed out of all recognition to Reid's record. It was painful trying to redraw the scene. Thank goodness he did not go to Sullom Voe, the capital of the oil industry in Shetland.

Heading for Dunrossness was a great relief.

JTR *It is a noteworthy fact that in all Dunrossness, an extensive parish, there is not a single house licensed to sell spirituous liquors. The peasantry of this district are superior to those of many parts of Shetland. Their crofts are better cultivated, and they are more diligent in the prosecution of the fishing. They use little carts, respectable ploughs, and decent spades. In a successful year they make a good livelihood by the fishing, and many have saved sums varying from £20 to £100. However, their calling exposes them continually to danger . . .*

Reid goes on to describe one of the all too frequent tragedies of *da haaf*, the offshore fishing grounds that could sometimes be as far as 50 miles distant from land. Sixareens, boats with six oarsmen, would set out in pairs. Weather judged fair from shore could change within

Scott's Jarlshoff —
— his fantastical name for Sumburgh Castle —

VIEW OF SUMBURGH.

minutes to gale-force winds once out at sea. Stones were ballast until the weight of fish replaced them. Tremendous skills and stamina were needed to survive such conditions, which could last for days at a time. Lines to be continually baited, many lost.

Such endurance for the sake of a catch of fish, a proportion of which was demanded by the landowner. The fishermen rented the lines from the landowner and any lost meant a fine.

*   *   *

Reid does not mention any particular village in the Dunrossness district but looking at the map he might well have walked through Scatness on his way to make his drawing of Fitful Head. There he might have heard a story of a miracle of the sea.

In late January of the year previous to Reid's visit the packet boat *Columbine*, owned by his young laird friend, set sail for Lerwick from Grutness with a sole Scatness passenger, Betty Mouat. All of 60 years old, a spinster, she was going to Lerwick to sell her shawls and see a doctor for reasons of ill health.

Three miles off Sumburgh, a sudden southeasterly blew up and part of the rigging broke free, knocking the skipper and mate overboard. The mate hauled himself aboard and along with the third member of the crew launched the small boat to save the skipper. Meanwhile the *Columbine*, uncontrolled, with wind in her sail, moved fast out of reach. The *Columbine* and her now very sole passenger headed out into the North Sea.

The skipper was never found. The crew got back to land but a fruitless search for the packet boat was abandoned.

Eight days later the *Columbine* was washed aground near Alesund in Norway, with Betty alive and relatively well on board. She had survived on a bottle of milk and some ship's biscuits. A heroine's welcome awaited her when she got home. Queen Victoria sent her admiration and £20.

Betty lived a further 30 years quietly knitting in Scatness and died at the age of 93.

*   *   *

JTR   *When at Sumburgh I rode occasionally to Sandlodge, and was ever most kindly entertained by John Bruce, Esq., and family.*

From thence I was rowed over to the island of Mousa, to get a sketch of the old castle, the most complete ruin of the period in Great Britain.

Reid did not always mention where hospitality was provided on his rambles, but he certainly did when it came to the houses of the rich and powerful.

*   *   *

Sandlodge, halfway between Sumburgh and Lerwick on the east coast of the mainland, was another 'stately pile' of Bruce masonry conveniently placed central to their other properties. Well preserved, it is now a private house belonging to descendants.

The copper mine established there in 1789 was flooded by the time Reid paid a visit but would open again in 1872. No doubt he and John Bruce, Esq., talked of this possibility, but more topical could have been the ongoing rumblings of discontent among Bruce's tenants.

Not only did a laird have the right to demand a share of the fish catch, but he also took his proportion of a whale hunt.

When a school of *Caain' Whales* – Pilot Whales – was sighted, it was every man to the boats to encircle the whales and drive them into a voe, the narrower the better, whereupon they were trapped

and killed, primarily for oil from the blubber.

One such hunt ended up in Channerwick Voe on Bruce's land. A Malcolm Mouat was authorised by the tenants to tell Bruce that they would keep the full share. 'He said he would see us in hell first,' was Mouat's reply to the men. The final threat was that their rents would go up or they would be evicted if they took the full share.

It would be a further 21 years before islanders would have security of tenure through the Crofters' Holding Act of 1886 and those men and their sons would take the laird to court after a similar confrontation and win the Hoswick Whale Case in that same year.

It's hard to imagine that Reid would not have known about these crises, as he socialised with landowners, yet he never comments. The price of hospitality? Or did he choose to be oblivious to it all, just dreaming of the next day's rambling?

*   *   *

My brush and sketchpad went on strike when I found out the only way to get to Mousa was to drive back down to Aithsvoe. Queues waited on the jetty to get aboard M/B *Solan IV,* a four-star Scottish Tourist Board tour vessel. The broch would be swarming with, dare I say, *tourists*. Oh! what snobbery – was I but not one of them? No.

One day I will go back out of season and accept that I will not hear the Storm Petrels chirruping in the walls of the broch.

Sumburgh House and Hotel

MELBY.

CHAPTER V

Papa Stour and the Missing Horn

By now I had given up keeping on a parallel sequence to Reid's ramblings. The engravings in the book led me on in the direction of Papa Stour. The small islands always calling.

There was time to get to Harry's legendary Emporium in Lerwick for a sleeping bag for Kia.

Sleeping in the back seat of a car by choice can be tolerable. By the second night I had discovered that the front passenger seat could be folded back quite flat. After days of often rough walking to find the exact spot of Reid's sketching stance, the accommodation was quite luxurious. And all a trial run for the soon to be mended Land Rover, which would sniff at the conventional nocturnal laybys of Kia.

I looked forward to that.

Nov much change

Melby

couldn't find the gothic rocks ...

JTR *. . . I reached Melby House, the delightful residence of R.T.C. Scott, Esq. of Melby, where, by kind invitation, I took up my abode. The house is built on a small promontory, and commands a magnificent view of the cliff scenery which bounds St Magnus Bay.*

I took up my abode there, too, parked close to the wall of the graveyard further up the hill where the view over Papa Stour to Canada and a setting sun in between was more magnificent.

Second son of the laird, Robert Thomas Charles, became an eminent naval doctor and only on the death of his brother took on the responsibility of the estate at the age of 48. He appears to have been an 'improver' compared to Bruce of Sumburgh and others,

possibly because of his profession furth of Shetland and not being involved with trade and manufacturing. He built new houses and gave a plot of land to the local teacher, Robert Jamieson, for a new school at Sandness.

When Douglas showed me the copy of *Art Rambles in Shetland* all those years ago, there was one sheet of a letter pasted inside. It was to Jamieson from Reid, dated London, June 16th 1869. It apologised for the possibility of not having replied to Jamieson's '*last kind letter*'. And continued: '*I have been quite rejoiced* [handwriting obscure] *to hear of your great quite unparalled* [*sic*] *success – you have indeed struck the nail on the head and hit the iron while it was hot.*'

How I would *love* to know to what that referred! Anything to do with the new school? By 1869 Jamieson, a respected educationalist in Scotland let alone Shetland, was at the height of his campaign for funding for the school. He had asked all teachers in Scotland to donate sixpence. Aided by correspondence with *The Scotsman* the simple idea caught on.

The last lines on the page explain Reid's purpose in writing: '*that my sister is to send you in my absence a copy of* 'Art Rambles' *which I hope you will get it safely and like it*'.

I would like to think Reid included a sixpence in the envelope.

*   *   *

Serendipity is the delight of research and, I hope, Dear Reader, as Reid would say, these digressions are of interest.

*   *   *

JTR   *On this estate . . . is the 'Holm of Collaster,' a small grassy islet situated in the middle of a loch. It is the haunt of myriads of wild fowl, as it is strictly preserved by the proprietor, and the nests are sometimes left undisturbed for several successive years. The Holm was last visited by the proprietor in May 1867, when eight hundred and eighty nine eggs were carried off. After having been boiled hard, they were, according to custom, distributed among friends in Shetland and elsewhere — one box having reached its destination in Cornwall with the contents perfectly fresh and good. With reference to the 'Preservation of Sea Birds Act', recently passed, it may be remarked that there was no perceptible diminution in the number of birds in the following year.*

I have a notion Reid was toadying to his host. To give Scott his due, he and Laurence Edmondston of Buness were wholly responsible for the salvation of the Great Skua, or *Bonxie*, which certainly was not nesting on the Holm, its numbers on the verge of extinction. Scott, posthumously, was given a medal by the Royal Zoological Society for his protection of the distinctive bird that I was to meet on Papa.

As in the Highlands and Islands, the Victorians came to Shetland to indulge in their wild game bloodbath and trophy hunting. Taxidermy was a growth industry. Ornithologists, to say nothing of naturalists, botanists, zoologists, geologists, mineralogists and all the other 'ists', were crawling over Shetland at that time. Laurence Edmondston had regular correspondence with Darwin; the isolation of the Shetland Isles of recurring interest to the great naturalist. And there was Reid in the middle of it all, with pen and sketchbook. How was *he* viewed? I imagine him listening politely to his hosts but longing for the next day's wild miles to explore on his own. A bit like myself.

Collaster was a quiet little loch with no '*wild bushes growing close to the water's edge*'. It was fringed with invasive Bogbean instead. There was no sign of nesting birds of any kind, not even a duck, on the pancake of an island. 'Used to be a tern colony,' said the local, come to see what I was up to. 'Bonxies destroyed 'em.'

JTR   *South from Melby, the rocks are abrupt in outline, rising in jagged peaks to a height of five or six hundred feet. At Deep Dale, the coast is very wild and desolate.*

The Melby man in blue overalls with his dog, dead rabbits over his shoulder, carefully put the safety catch on his gun as he bent over to look at Reid's engraving of the coast at Deep Dale. 'Huxter road end is the nearest you'll get by car. Then it's a muckle walk.'

It was a windless evening and the moor of peat hags seemed to stretch for ever, with the headland getting no nearer. It was ten o'clock by the time I got to the edge of the cliff, the sun still not set. Nor would it. Reid's cauldron of stiff waves thrashed by an offshore wind gently flapped on the photocopied page in my hand. Pink westering clouds hung in the sky above a peach-pink horizon line. I was the only person in the world.

*   *   *

For Reid, every voe along the coastline had a boatman, often to be searched for, who could be hired for some *siller*. Thus Reid sailed to Papa Stour direct from Melby. I had to travel east a considerable distance along the switchback, twisting road to West Burrafirth for the little car ferry that serves the short distance to Papa Stour. Once again the ridiculously cheap charges. But as I learned, this economic link with the island brings mixed blessings.

As I waited and watched early on the pier, the day started with

THE COAST—DEEP DALE, NEAR MELBY.

South of Melby

Deep Dale Coast.

the crew readying up for the ferry's first crossing to Papa and the powerful engine roar of fishing boats as they headed out the Firth past Galta Stack and the Riv Skerries.

Leaning against an old roofless stone store, I witnessed another start to the day's survival. With high-speed zig-zagging aerobatics, two Great Black-backed gulls hounded a hoodie crow, carrying one of their eggs in its beak, down into the building where it proceeded to crack open the shell and gorge on the foetus. Surrounded and protected by a nettled heap of old creels and floats, the hoodie, hunched against the screaming attacks of the parents, calmly finished its repast before flying up and over the wall, the gulls chasing until the three of them were far out of sight over the bay.

Tenements of starlings went busily in and out the cracks in the old wall quite unperturbed by the commotion. It all happened very quickly.

*   *   *

There was one other passenger on the ferry. Jane was coming back home for the weekend from her work in Lerwick. She had had a job in the island school and when the last two children left the school was closed.

'There are only 22 people living here. Other crofters like me have to commute to the mainland for work, staying away all week.'

How convenient the car ferry, I suggested, especially at £4.50 a crossing. But there was the rub; easy access to and from the mainland had reduced the crofters' working week on the island to weekends only. The Crofters Commission was querying their validity. There was talk of their possible definition as 'absentee crofters' and all that that entailed. Shades of nineteenth century overlordship?

As Reid perambulated over the island he would have seen many of the 360 residents thralled to the prosperous fishing industry at its peak on Papa.

JTR   *. . . an island rich in subjects for the pencil, and rich as being peculiarly adapted both by its position and natural construction for fishing purposes. It is near to the ling fishing-grounds, and its shores are indented with deep voes, which form excellent and safe harbours, in which hundreds of boats and small smacks could be safely moored. It appears immense shoals of herring pass from* *north to south near its shores, almost annually in July, and are frequently driven by the numerous saith, their voracious persecutors, into creeks and voes.*

The curing station was run by Adie and Sons from Voe on the mainland. His shop sold rope and paint, biscuits and tea. The latter was an addiction all over Shetland, especially among the poor.

*   *   *

It was a warm, windy day. Papa Stour is a flat little island and I looked forward to an easy tramp in search of Reid's dramatic discoveries – the Horn of Papa on the other side of the island and, on the way, '*Christie's Hole*'. I was told to go by the coast and not directly across because of the nesting bonxies.

*   *   *

There is a scattering of houses up from the pier and the excavated remains of Duke Håkon's thirteenth-century *stofa*, reconstructed with logs brought from Norway and an outer skin of drystane walling built by Norwegian craftsmen. Shetland dykers finished the stone walling and it is interesting to see the difference in style.

Further along the mile-and-a-half's worth of road I passed the deserted school and scrunched over the gravelled airstrip. Shetland Isles Council serves its remote communities well for transport.

Now I was onto the open moor. Keeping inland from the cliff edges, I soon found with a gasp of warranted horror a vast hole in my path that opened into turquoise water gently surging 100 feet below. Kirstan's Hole was the collapsed roof of a sea cave that stretched nearly 1,000 feet inland to where seals rest on shelves deep underground. There are several more of these long caves with smaller inland openings on the route to the Horn. On days of storms the water spouts are tremendous, they say. Kirstan's must be like looking down into a cauldron of hell. Summer or winter, the grass slopes round the edges are slippery. I still recoil and my stomach churns at the memory of that first sighting despite the holiday brochure blue of the sea so far below.

Reid's engraving of the jutting headland of the Horn looks like a weird giant-sized horse, neck and forelegs down in the sea, back legs attached to the land, a tiny hunchbacked rider atop. The latter being the 'horn'. Or maybe it is more like a rhinocerous horn . . .

When I got there, according to the map, I had my suspicions. Had I caught my mentor out at last? Secretly, I'd always hoped for such an exposure. I'd forgiven him his Romantic and Gothic interpretations up till now, but this headland just did not exist. Such exaggeration for effect!

The peculiar atmosphere of Papa, which I was beginning to sense, must have affected him, too.

I started to doubt the OS map and spent many an hour tracking and backtracking this fantastical coast of pink cliffs and stacks dotted with nesting fulmars. Sizeable lumps of shattered Old Red Sandstone flung upwards by storms were scattered inland over the flat-topped cliff edges to a distance of over 260 feet. By Loch Aesha and the remains of tiny Trowie corn mills at the back of beyond, the stones were more than 300 feet inland which surely could only have been dropped like pink flinty meteorites from the sky, so unbelievable is the savage strength of the sea.

All the while the grey blue outline of Foula teased me from the west. Another strange island, they said.

Passive bonxies stood like big brown ducks on stilts of legs watching me. I was late and decided to set off cross country to catch the last ferry. Bonxies nest inland and what a welcome there was for me when I got to the middle of the island. The locals were right. I spent the whole journey one OS map clamped to my head, continually waving another in the air. It is the eery silence of their hundred-mile-an-hour approach from behind that deceives when you think they have gone. All in all, Papa Stour had quite shaken me.

Back in civilisation I collapsed in the little waiting room at the pier. Neat and tidy, it had a cheery notice in amongst the tourist brochures. 'Help yourself to a cup of tea or coffee.' On a table there was an electric kettle and jars for the tea and coffee. Both were empty and there were no cups or mugs. Somehow it summed up the air of desuetude I felt on Papa; good intentions but the energy to carry them out difficult to find.

A sparrow had got in the open window; with difficulty and a tea towel, I helped it to freedom.

JTR *In Papa Stour, as elsewhere, the sparrows are very destructive to the corn, and the Papa Stourians believed that the beadle of the*

The Horn-less Papa

kirk had the power of 'telling' the sparrows away so as to never return, for which they paid him a fee. The 'Sparrow-Beadle' still lives on the island, though he has not been employed in the 'sparrow-telling' capacity for a few years. It must have been rather an amusing sight to have seen and heard him going round the cornfields using a variety of gesticulations, crying "Coosh-sh-sh, Hoosh-sh-sh awa' fra dis toon, and never come again." The sparrows must have found his annual visit much more enjoyable than the never-failing presence of a scarecrow.

'So how was your day?' asked the ferry engineer up for a breath of fresh air as we made the return journey to West Burrafirth. I told him the frustration of not finding the horn. He looked at the picture. 'Oh! that front bit and the Horn broke off in a big storm way back in '53!' And he took my pencil and drew a line through the bizarre image.

And that explains why you will never find any reference to the

THE HORN OF PAPA AND VAE SKERRIES.

Horn of Papa as a visitor attraction in later tourist publications. It is just another headland.

My apologies to Mr Reid. Vindicated, I let him travel on his way southwards.

*   *   *

JTR *On my way to Reawick I called at the manse of Watsness and passed a pleasant day with the hospitable clergyman; and on reaching Reawick itself, I was most kindly entertained by Andrew Umphray, Esq., and family, who aided me in appreciating very thoroughly the beauties of that charming locality.*

Papa Stour
Hornless
Headland

MANSE OF WATSNESS.

The substantial manse of Watsness had been quite recently built when Reid visited. The parish of Walls and Sandness was vast and included Papa Stour and Foula. Whatever went wrong, ecclesiastically, the minister left quite soon after Reid's visit and it became a tenant farm.

In the days of sea travel, the area would have been alive with people but today the long, thin inland road from Melby has so many deserted ruins dotted on the hillsides. The road narrows to where it ends at the tired, lonely nineteenth-century *Haa* surrounded by high drystane dykes that stretch across fields as they have done for over a hundred years.

As I knocked to ask if I could go into one of the fields to get the right angle for Reid's illustration, Magnus opened the faded door.

The old man, bent and gentle with the years, said, 'But

everyone calls me Sonny. It was what my mother called me.'
Somehow I just knew the spelling of his name was 'Sunny' and his
mother still lived in his heart.

Three generations of his family had lived and been born in the
house. Now he was the last, tending his cattle, and the dog that
seemed as old as himself. Everything around was so deserted. Sunny
had never married. A nephew and cousin helped out at busy times.
He gallantly insisted on opening the gate to the field, and the cows,
as gentle as he, came sidling round us, placidly chewing his anorak.

The day was still. As I stood there sketching, the phenomenal
natural violence and human exhaustion on Papa seemed very far
away at the end of the road to Watsness.

*   *   *

Reawick is a long haul south and east from Watsness on foot, but
Reid was a Victorian. I wanted to head that way, too. Lerwickwards,
eventually. The Land Rover was ready.

Reid was certainly introducing me to his network of influential
families in Shetland. Mrs Umphrey was the daughter of William
Hay of the shipping business Hay and Ogilvie based in Lerwick.

House hidden by sheds. Reawick

REAWICK.

Raewick

Hay's Dock is the present appropriately historical site of the new Shetland Museum and Archives.

Reid's idyllic portrayal of Raewick was all there save for a few more houses and the many agricultural buildings, sadly, but practically, surrounding the old house built in 1730. The home of farming descendants, Raewick House is one of the very few *Haas* of Reid's Rambles that continues a resident family link with the past. Many of the others are now public buildings or holiday homes.

*   *   *

Grooming her pony in the yard, the young Hay daughter was intrigued by the old engraving. There was the mill in the foreground still standing, and leaning against the wall the iron frame of the wooden wheel that Reid had sketched 143 years previously.

I had to sneak a peek into the mill. The wooden threshing equipment still stood and the gearing cogs were rustily attached through the green moulded wall to where the waterwheel had once turned outside. The millpond behind was empty but the burn still flowed down to the sea.

*   *   *

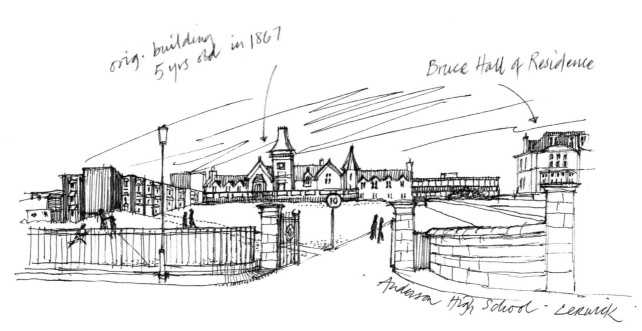

orig. building 5 yrs old in 1867

Bruce Hall of Residence

Anderson High School - Lerwick

THE ANDERSON INSTITUTE, LERWICK.

Having returned Kia to her compound at Northern Ferries Terminal in Lerwick, I had time to wander before the overnight luxury 'cruise' on the *Hjaltland* back to Scotland and recovery of my faithful old set of wheels.

Hidden in amongst nearby industrial sprawl is the Böd of Gremista Museum, birthplace of Arthur Anderson, born 1792, son of a fish curer. Aged 16 with basic education, he joined the Royal Navy, ending up in his 20s destitute in London before becoming a clerk in a shipping company and finally co-founding the P&O Navigation Co. in 1837. On return to Shetland he created *The Shetland Journal*

> . . . to diffuse among the peasantry of Shetland such infor-
> mation as shall tend to enlarge their ideas and stimulate
> their industry . . . to expose the unjust treatment which
> Shetland has experienced ever since its annexation to
> Britain.

Anderson had big radical ideas and was Liberal Democrat MP for Orkney and Shetland from 1847 to 1852. The Anderson Institute Secondary School in Lerwick still stands as evidence of his philanthropy, especially in education for the youth of Shetland.

'A Shetlander, and nane o' thae Scotch bodies!' as the ferryman's wife on Bressay would have proudly said.

CHAPTER VI

To Hillswick without Kate

Returning to Shetland with the Land Rover a few days later on the now familiar ferry, I could get a berth. After the customary dinner in the Ladeberry, it was dark enough for the North Ronaldsay lighthouse to welcome me back as it beamed the memory of its light towards Fair Isle. A platinum grey, waveless, broaching sea stretched to a pencil-line horizon. A hint of red in the pencil stroke. Shepherd's delight, maybe.

Early next morning Lerwick woke to continuing grey as *Hjaltland* slid towards the terminal. The Shetland Museum and Archives at Hay's Dock viewed from the sea had more than a hint of the Sydney Opera House. The burgundy wood facings of the extension to the traditional pier stores were configured in the shape of the very sails of the smacks that Reid had travelled on from island to island.

Much as I enjoyed wandering about the quaint alleyways and vennels of Lerwick, coffees at the Peerie Shop and especially the treasure trove of the Archives at Hay's Dock, I drove straight off the ferry this time and followed Reid north and westwards to the village of Hillswick. It is on the peninsula of North Mavine, tenuously linked to the mainland by a stitch of land.

JTR *Thither bound, I left Lerwick on pony-back. Kate, the handsome gray mare kindly placed at my disposal for the journey, was grand-daughter to a fine Arabian war-horse, presented, after having seen considerable service, to the late Sir Arthur Nicolson. Hence the origin of the famous breed of Fetlar ponies.*

According to the New Statistical Account of 1845, Sir Arthur Nicolson brought cross-breed sheep to Fetlar that did not thrive and spread scab on the island. Kate must be proof that his other novel introduction of an Arab stallion courtesy of General Bolívar of

Venezuela had survived. It was crossed with an Orkney garron and stalwart Kate the result. One wonders if the famous Byerly Turk might have been involved as well. Reid was riding equine history.

There is no word for pony in the Old Norse dialect of Shetland. A horse is either big or *muckle*, wee or *peerie*.

JTR *Two gentlemen galloped past us mounted on spirited brown shelties, and Kate started in hot pursuit, while I, being quite unaccustomed to this sort of exercise, found ample occupation in keeping my seat . . .*

I followed comfortably behind in the customised Countess, for that was her name, on the broad sweeping road that dipped and curved with excellent cambers, Radio 3 soaring out the windows and over the hills.

JTR *For several miles a hilly and torturous road is followed, passing numerous lochs on either hand, until we arrive at the 'Lang Kaim', a dismal valley where, three years ago, nought met the eye for more than six dreary miles but a boundless expanse of peat moss, with no human dwelling, however humble, to break the stillness of the scene. Now, however, at the entrance to the Kaim, and close to the road, a little inn is erected, where Kate had corn, and I a considerable tea.*

There was the lonely 'inn' halfway along the never-ending valley, with miles of uninhabited moorland stretching on either side.

Charlotte told me that it had been run for many years as Sandwater Hotel, the name for the little loch nearby. 'In the days of horses and carts. I think I have got photos somewhere . . .'

Her family had bought the empty hotel in the mid '20s after 'drink, in the way of some publicans, caused ruin'. The croft attached was the mainstay and the house was never used as an inn or hotel again. 'They say it was a great meeting place for cattle sales in the days of the inn. It's just called the Halfway House now.'

Gently spoken and now 'getting on', Charlotte told me she lived alone . She had looked after her mother for many years. Her mother was now dead. The sheep in the field were just pets, she said. Charlotte did not want any more lambs.

Eventually the old photos were found after every drawer and

cupboard was raked through. It was important to Charlotte that I saw them.

Somehow, with the main road north just over the fence constantly streaming with container lorries, tankers, tourist traffic and commuters, the dim sitting room and its tentative little peat fire in the Halfway House was sanctuary for Charlotte, Reid and myself.

I always kept a box of little presents to hand for times like this. The Shetland Soap Co. had stocked it up last time I had been in Lerwick. Shelves of sweet smelling soaps were labelled with couthie Shetland names for flowers and herbs and seaweed.

I gave Charlotte the soap with the label *smooriekins*. I had chosen it in the shop for the comfort of the sound it made.

'What does it mean?' I asked.

'Kisses,' she replied, shyly.

*   *   *

Voe lies at the end of the long '*dreary*' valley and at the head of Olna Firth. It is a pleasant surprise cresting the hill to look down on the attractive village below – except for the eyesore of the electricity exchange at the summit, fretting its view. The long inlet of the voe is dotted with rows and rows of mussel farm floats. A latter-day industry replaces that observed by Reid.

JTR   *At the top of this voe are built a few houses, with slated roofs; and the artificial beaches adjacent indicate one of the most extensive fish curing establishments in the country.*

Voe, a backwater of rural poverty, had become famous because of the entrepreneurship of a young 15-year-old lad called Thomas Adie, who started his career by delivering groceries and subsequently created business enterprises that dominated life for miles around for over 150 years.

Faroese boats landed their cod catches for drying on the man-made beaches of stones, as did the Shetlanders their herring and ling. Fish curing was not the only activity of Thomas Adie and, latterly, Sons; a large shop, farming and textile manufacturing provided much needed labour in a district that had been decimated by ruthless clearance at the beginning of the nineteenth century. The Adie fish curing empire stretched from Papa Stour in the west to

Whalsey in the east and the capital of Lerwick in the south.

The '*few houses, with slated roofs*' were the new dwellings of distinction built by the Adie family. Voe House, Bellevue and the Manse are sited above the reclaimed artificial beaches. An Adie still lives in one of them.

The houses command fine views over the jetty, with its new stone breakwater sheltering small fishing boats and yachts. The old sail loft and salt store are transformed into a camping *böd*; the characterful and aged Voe Pub opposite has no doubt given sustenance and solace to generations of Voerians, as Reid would designate them. All is in keeping with the charmingly eccentric locals who patronise the hostelry today. One is a Belgian who 'comes and goes' and lives in a mussel-raft work hut moored near the shore. A chimney indicates a stove installed on the verandah that surrounds the open water within the hut, which also houses a bed. The Belgian is building a sixareen boat. 'Where better,' he emphasises, 'to build a boat but on the water.'

I discreetly fled the mounting conviviality and generosity of the Voe Pub. All of Olnafirth had been put on the alert, the telephone in action to find *the* historian of Voe. It was arranged that I would meet her the next morning.

That night in a perfect, hidden site on the old road by the edge of the Firth and sheltered by embankments for the new road behind, I reflected on the balance between individual research for my project and too local involvement. Up till now I had been able to move on like a butterfly, sipping the nectar until I had had my fill of flavours. The thought of an appointment on the morrow filled me with dread. Would my butterfly approach be unmasked?

Lorene could not have been more helpful and interested in the mission I had taken upon myself. She had written a book with a wealth of photos about the Adies and their influence on Voe. The stone beaches had to be created because the natural indentation of little voes and shingle beaches were of no use for drying fish. Men gathered flat stones, the bigger the better, and laid them inland in 'fields'.

Subsequently the fishing industry collapsed but Adie and Sons were prepared for the eventuality and developed textiles and knitting. The stones were used to build houses for workers. Lorene's grandparents had been employed in the industry. She herself had become a teacher but was now retired.

If only young Thomas had lived to enjoy the story of the contract won by his firm in 1952 to supply 24 fine Shetland wool (plucked from the sheep's neck) jumpers for Hunt's Everest Expedition. The New Zealanders, Hillary and Lowe – or the sherpas – were not measured for the order.

Olnafirth, I learned, was the correct name for the village. Voe was the crofting area where the first Adie, an ex-naval surgeon and merchant, father of Thomas, had bought land. The naval surgeon appears to have been of doubtful integrity in relation to the ladies and it fell to young Thomas to make his own way in life. Originally a farming and merchant business was established at the Voe croft but soon enterprise after enterprise gave the name to the whole district. 'It's all happening at Voe' was the message being spread around, bringing folk hopeful of work.

It must have been the Sullom Voe of its time.

*   *   *

Reid briefly comments in passing on the industrial developments he sees on his travels, preferring to wax lyrical about the landscape that is his prime source of inspiration. Was not the activity and smell at Voe not quite overwhelming?

Was that why he quickly moved on? Heading for '*hospitable shelter*' six miles distant at Busta, '*which has been for more than three centuries the residence of the Gifford family – a fine old mansion-house, surrounded by a goodly array of trees, stunted in height, but having trunks of from two to three feet in circumference. On a fine evening, when reflected in the voe on whose sweeping banks it is built, it looks extremely picturesque, somewhat like a lordly mansion by the banks of a Highland loch*'.

The butterfly moved on to Busta, too, for hospitable shelter.

The Rocks family, who run Busta House as a hotel, had invited me to stay. Their daughter and one of my grandsons are at the Aberdeen Music School and word had got out about Sam's art-rambling grannie – no doubt spread by Sam himself.

Veronica and Joe were adamant that not only I have dinner with them but also I was to stay as long as I liked. I assured them of the comforts of the Countess. But did I have a whiff on me of the Voe of 1867?

Not after the longest, luxuriously bubbled bath I'd had since

BUSTA.

leaving home in early May. It was now well into June and I have to admit the spirits were flagging. The kindness of the Rocks almost broke my resolve to carry on. Oh! to just be on holiday like the other guests . . . to be looked after.

Wandering about the rooms in the older part of Busta House, with architectural features unchanged from Reid's time, I was reminded of my underlying quest – to find some reference to his existence, other than the book that had dictated my days for so long. I'd found a letter. A faded book on a shelf, a print – an original! – on a wall?

Having no success trawling through the old library, I became fascinated by the history of the Giffords, who haunt the house in more ways than one.

The earliest part of the house was built in 1588. Around about 1714 it was extended by Thomas Gifford. He had married the daughter of a Scalloway landowner and his future was assured. He established a fishing station like many of his peers and made a fortune as a fish exporter and merchant.

By 1748, the now Sir Thomas and Lady Gifford had ambitions for their 30-year-old eldest son and heir to get married. But unbeknownst to them, John, six months previously, had secretly married Barbara Pitcairn, his mother's maid companion, who was an orphaned relative of minor importance.

In May of that year, John, his three brothers, a tutor and a boatman set off on a calm evening to visit relatives at Wethersta on the other side of Busta Voe. They never came back. Only the body of John and the tutor were dredged up. Barbara, hoping to console the Giffords at the loss of four sons, told them of her marriage and that she was pregnant. She was totally rejected and banished from Busta. But the baby, a son called Gideon, was claimed by the Giffords and was especially cherished by his grandfather. Barbara only saw her son once, when he was seven years old.

Once an adult, Gideon's inheritance was contested by a cousin and so ensued 93 years of law suits that ultimately bankrupted the estate. In the interval, however, Gideon lived a life of great style. Busta was open house. He died in 1811. By 1832, the final contest for the estate between Arthur, his son, and an Ollaberry Gifford came to a legal head; Arthur, impoverished, would only keep the title of laird in his lifetime. At his death in 1836 the estate was conveyed to trustees. And so the last Laird of Busta was laid to rest in Voe churchyard.

Buness

U.P. CHURCH AND MANSE, OLLABERRY.

Reid's host at Busta would have been a Thomas Gifford ('other side of the blanket', I was informed), who was factor to the estate for 42 years until his death in 1899 at 80 years old.

Barbara Pitcairn has never been at rest. She wanders the corridors looking for her baby son. Guests have seen her.

Other accounts have it that it is Lady Gifford who wails from room to room. In the jacket of her son's drowned body she found the marriage certificate, witnessed by two of John's brothers and a minister. This she hid to deny Barbara any inheritance.

*   *   *

orig. Free Church
Then church of
Scotland

Now a store

Tide out

Ollaberry

Next morning after a deep sleep in a four poster bed that Barbara and Lady Gifford kindly tiptoed past in the *wee sma' hours*, I was on the trail again. Like Kate, I had been fed and watered, but unlike her I had a misty start to the day with the promise of the sun burning through. This regular weather pattern is common in Orkney and Shetland and to a lesser extent in the Hebrides in spring and summer. The *haar* is created by cold air moving over warm sea or land. Another theory has it that when kelp seaweed is exposed to strong sunlight it releases particles of iodine that become water vapour. But whatever the reason, it seems to cling longer in Shetland.

JTR   *Next day, in spite of all the kind solicitations of my host not to venture out in such weather, I mounted to ride to Hillswick. The wind was furious, and my hat blew away beyond hope of recovery when at Mavis Grind, a romantic spot where the mainland is almost rent in twain, and a narrow band of twenty or thirty feet alone divides the Atlantic Ocean from the North Sea . . . Poor Kate was sadly tortured by the pelting showers; so much so, that sometimes she would stand stock still, utterly unable to proceed . . . I dismounted, shouldered my baggage, and led Kate, who now willingly followed me with her head close under my lee side.*

Poor Kate indeed. Her blue blood the bluer for her experience. When Reid reached the comfort of the Hillswick fire, '*for the fire is a welcome friend in Shetland all the year round*', he says no more about Kate and one wonders at her fate. Like bicycles in Bruges, she would be stabled until the next traveller came along.

For the most part I had good weather in Shetland. The £15 sleeping bag from Harry's was ever warm and cosy on the platform at the back of the Countess even when the early morning mist opaqued the windows. I did have one day of torrential rain. It passed with pleasant reading and, conveniently within signal range, listening to Radio 4 and Radio Shetland. The cigarette lighter socket boiled the little kettle for tea. Kate would not have been able to give me horsepower better than this.

I overnighted in the layby at Mavis Grind and wished for a wild storm to brew up from the west just to watch Atlantic waves arching over the road and crashing into the North Sea. The width of the short isthmus that carries the road on towards Hillswick is about 100 feet and it is possible to fling a stone from one shore to the other.

It was common practice in the days of sail and oar to use Mavis Grind as a shortcut from St Magnus Bay to Sullom Voe and beyond. Barbara Johnson tells of her husband's family leaving Papa Stour on a February dawn, three years before Reid and Kate struggled past, in two sixareens, heading for Otterswick many sea miles north and east on the island of Yell. The family consisted of a father, mother, three-year-old daughter and thirteen-month-old baby (the husband-to-be). Also in one of the boats were two cows and fodder enough to keep them 'till grass came'. All unloaded on the west shore, the sixareens then hauled across the isthmus and everything reloaded on the east shore. It was 11 p.m. by the time they got to Otterswick. The plaque at the side of the road does not give any reason for the marathon journey. A clearance or just a flitting?

*   *   *

There was a still air about Hillswick in the Saturday late afternoon. Still, not as in just windless, but in a waiting stillness. A sort of High Noon hazy heat. The walled garden to the front of Hillswick House sheltered climbing plants by the main door. The wall continued along the road, protecting a bountiful vegetable garden. A newly tarred work-aday forecourt stretched to the shore, fine mesh fishing nets mounded by the gravel and buttercup edge of a new sea wall. Hillswick House was still involved with the sea.

A base for the Hanseatic League traders, the original fishing *böd* was taken over by the Giffords in the early 1700s. By the mid nineteenth century, John Anderson, another Busta estate factor, had built the house that quietly sits by the shore today. Reid doesn't mention names when he visits the *Haas* if the landowner is not in residence. Anderson, however, also built a shop, post office and public house, numerous cottages for workers and his fast expanding family. Perhaps the welcome fire in the parlour was in the pub.

Hillswick must have been a busy place. It was a key port for the west coast link with Scalloway. Isolated like the North Isles, the road system was in its infancy and only in the south. Maybe this accounted for my impression of a lingering Wild West atmosphere. Although those pioneering days were long gone and a B road comes to its door, Hillswick, still mainland Shetland, just, was far removed from the pioneering-in-reverse *hamefarin* crowds in Lerwick.

Jan came out of one of the outbuildings by the walled garden. Did I want to see the seal pups? Hillswick House is still very much linked to the sea. Here is the Hillswick Wildlife Sanctuary.

It was founded in 1987 when Jan carried in her first seal pup, stranded on the foreshore. The cooperage where the herring was salted in barrels is the outbuilding where sick, orphaned and injured seals and otters are cared for. Word soon spread. Jan never quite knows what wounded or ailing creatures will turn up at the cooperage – from hedgehogs to turtles – but the main priority is the seals and the otters.

Nemo was five months premature when he was saved. The other pup had just been born and caught in time before a Black Back had pecked out its eyes. Both pups squiggled and slithered towards Jan, black pools of liquid liquorice eyes beseeching the bottle. 'Every four hours. Just like a human baby,' said Jan. She has the milk sent from Denmark. 'Works like no other.' The frail little pups started sucking each other once their feed was over.

The St Magnus Bay Hotel is prominently situated up the hill behind Hillswick House. White wood clad, three storeys high and verandah'd, it invited inspection. What a delight! The Wild West again! Inside, old brown varnished wood-lined walls were jammed with faded photos and mementoes of its Edwardian heyday. A framed picture in the porch of a row of white-aproned and frilly-headbanded maids awaited guests. The curlicued piano in the hall called out for the honkytonk to begin and saloon ladies to swan down the stairs into the vast dining room crowned with equally vast chandeliers hanging from the panelled roof.

The building was manufactured in Norway in 1900 and shipped over in kit form to Hillswick for the North of Scotland Orkney and Shetland Steam Navigation Company, who ran the vital shipping service from Scrabster on mainland Scotland to Stromness on Orkney and on to Scalloway on Shetland. It was to be the company's land flagship for the growing hotel resort business.

Over the years the property deteriorated, despite a brief enlivening at the beginning of 'the Oil' and then subsided to rot in its memories. The recently new owners have inherited a Forth Road Bridge undertaking. I wish them well but hope that they won't lose the genuine idiosyncratic heart of the building, dusty and a bit frayed at the edges though it may be.

At the expense of disbelief, I have to finally and honestly prove my laboured analogy of Hillswick to be true. Into the early evening still of that windless day came the Posse. In minibus after minibus the young from the whole of Shetland, it seemed, tumbled out onto the grass in front of the hotel, ordering drinks with thirst enough for the Last Chance Saloon in Kansas. Earrings longer than skirts, skyscraper shoes and sparkle shadowed eyes took over the hotel garden, its tables and chairs. And that was the boys.

It was the bride's hen party. But the cockerels were there, too. Everyone was clad in silver except for the bridegroom's puce pink froufrou skirt. I remembered noticing the extensive adult fancy dress section of the Party Shop in Lerwick. Shetlanders obviously love dressing up and not just for *Up Helly Aa*.

What would Mr Reid have thought?

He chose to leave all society behind and walk out to Hillswick Ness and sketch Rona's Hill. At midnight.

JTR *The sun having dipped behind Rona, still cast a bright radiance over the sky, reflecting a mellow, luminous, silvery light, which gilded the glassy surface of the voe . . . Light thickened, and the mist which had hitherto crested the fair summit of Rona now floated across the horizon on the morning breeze: touches of sunlight gilded the clouds and more distant hills, as the orb of the day rose resplendent, and decked the dew-clad landscape with a glittering robe lustrous with liquid diamonds.*

No, I could never rise, like Reid's sun, or from my sleeping bag, to such hyperbole. My comparison was executed the next morning after all the glasses had been cleared.

* * *

It took several days to walk the cliff coastline of St Magnus Bay. Starting from the sea pink drifts atop Hillswick Ness, round the apricot granite and red porphyry Heads of Grochen and The Neap, dropping to the south shore of Eshaness before rising to the lighthouse and on to the Wagnerian-sounding Grind of the Navir, the weirdest of cliff formations, the playground of sea giants.

The pinnacle stacks of the Drongs and the Dore Holm in the bay are part of the playground: the Drongs the top spikes of a dragon climbing frame and the Dore Holm a feeding heffalump to ride on.

DORE HOLM—NEAR TANGWICK, NORTH MAVEN.

But, one evening, looking over the mirror-sheened bay from Stenness, the Drongs were washed burnt sienna from a setting sun and could have been a becalmed flotilla of nineteenth-century sailing smacks.

Tracks that led to nowhere with not a habitation or soul in sight were my evening retreat. To quote Reid quoting the poet Crabbe:

> I love to walk where none had walk'd before,
> About the rocks that ran along the shore;
> Or far beyond the sight of men to stray,
> And take my pleasure when I lost my way.

The rhyming couplets get in the way but he has perfectly said it for the three of us.

*   *   *

The Drongs.
-St. Magnus Bay .

· Dore Holm ·   · North Maven ·

Reid has a detailed description of the fishing station at Stenness, where there were 'rows of huts or lodges, *ten or twelve of them built in a block, having side-walls instead of gables in common. So small are they, that they suggest dog-kennels rather than human habitations; yet in each a boat's crew dwell for a few months in summer, generally sleeping with their clothes on, among straw, away from their homes and snug box-beds. Their wives, sisters, or daughters visit them once a-week to get the cod-heads, small fish, and skate, for home consumption. The drying beaches were strewn with fish; and the boats, having been two nights at sea, had returned with splendid catches of cod and ling, which were being duly weighed, gutted and salted by a staff of men and boys engaged for this service.'*

Stenness was one of Shetland's busiest *haaf* stations. Forty sixareens were based there. Cheynes of Tangwick *Haa*, married onto Hays, were the landlords. From 1840, they were non resident and living in Edinburgh. They were not typical landowners; they had a good reputation and not just because they gave a bottle of whisky for the midsummer *Johnsmas Foy* celebration suppers. Maybe because they were not resident like Scott of Melby and maybe because their factor was a decent man and the islanders got fair payment for the fish landed. I'd like to think so.

Unlike Mavis Grind, the Grind of the Navir was a couple of rough miles on from the road end at the lighthouse. No habitation there for the Countess. But like Mavis Grind the weather was sunny and the wind a zephyr. No giants at play in the sea.

It took two attempts on two separate days to find the Grind. Reid's engraving took on the frustrations of his Horn of Papa. Had the Gateway of the Grind collapsed into the sea, too? I had no other visual references. I had also, for the first time, not taken the OS map. The other few and far between cliff walkers didn't even know the name. They were 'just out for a walk'. With the sea so calm, there was not even the hope of a marker of skyward spray.

Without the map I had not plodded the full length of the coastline. Just before the Head of Stanshi was the opening. An elevated platform many feet above sea level, framed by a 'gateway' in the cliffs, stretches all of 150 feet inland and is scattered with not rocks but blocks of stone weighing tons. I measured many from two to four feet by one foot. They are broken off the cliffs by the force of gigantic storm waves and flung up through the opening. Offshore wave heights can reach 60 feet before they crash into *da Grind*.

The Drongs. Drifts of Sea Pinks
Hillswick Ness

STENNIS

The ready-made masoned stones wait for the Romans to build a Coliseum or an amphitheatre of colonnaded columns to surround a Lido already hollowed out on the platform. That summer's day the water left there from a previous storm was warm as a toddlers' pool, the giants asleep deep down below.

stone ruins of base of wooden huts. ?

Böd repointed Roof next ?

sea facing v. orange/yell. lichen

Stenness

Banks of pebbles to the door.

Stenness.

GRIND OF THE NAVIR—NORTH MAVINE.

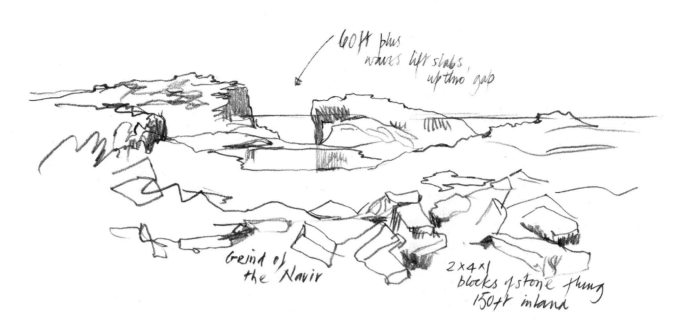

60ft plus
waves lift slabs,
up thro' gap

Grind of
the Navir

2×4×1
blocks of stone flung
150ft inland

The Grind of the Navir.

·So many cloudless days·
~ after the morning
haar

FOULA, FROM THE HILL ABOVE SCALLOWAY.

CHAPTER VII

The Other Edge of the World

Lawrence Durrell in his book *Reflections of a Marine Venus* defined the word *islomania* as 'a rare affliction of the spirit' and *islomanes* as sufferers from this powerful attraction to islands.

Extreme *islomanes* head for St Kilda in the Hebrides. The Edge of the World. *Ultima Thule*. But many other islands compete for these titles. The Roman historian Tacitus maintained that *ultima Thule* could be seen from Orkney. Shetland? Others believed it was to be found in the Faroes, Iceland, or Greenland. The Scottish Gaelic for Iceland is *Innes Tile* – Isle of Thule.

Us *islomaniacs* all have our own idea. In Shetland, it is Foula.

*   *   *

Foula

For six years, the film-maker Michael Powell kept a newspaper cutting of the 1930 evacuation of Hirta, the only inhabited island of the St Kilda group. Definitely an *islomane*, he long held the ambition to make a film about the historic event on the actual island. The owner, the Earl of Dumfries, and subsequently the Marquis of Bute, would not give permission. He wanted the island to become a bird sanctuary.

Foula was substituted for Powell's film, which was called *Edge of the World*. In the days before an air service and only a small boat link to the mainland, cast and crew had to be handpicked and as committed as Powell for the four isolated months of filming.

Many of the islanders took part in the film but the island star has to be the *peerie* mongrel collie that tries to save his master's life on the crags. The dog became so attached to one of the crew – or vice versa – that the two of them left the island together at the end of the project.

When the film came out in 1937, it was well received in America and Powell's name in the film world was made. His profits were greatly diminished, however, by the Earl of Dumfries suing for use of the name of Hirta for Foula. Powell won the case but had to pay costs.

*   *   *

I decided to take the little eight-seater plane from Tingwall to Foula. 'Once the fog clears,' smiled the pilot from Botswana, who had met and married a lass from Scalloway. 'Only takes 15 minutes.'

The boat crossing every second day from Walls is a couple of hours but, like Fair Isle, timetabled by sea conditions. The waves that reach Foula have the whole of the North Atlantic to build up momentum.

JTR *Desiring to visit this 'Isle of the sea' – the supposed Ultima Thule of the Romans – I got on board the* Swallow, *a trading sloop. A favourable breeze wafted us thither . . . and as dusk faded into night we anchored at a small geo . . . The teacher, a very versatile genius, who had just returned from the piltock-fishing, rowed us ashore in his boat. A very versatile genius indeed. He reads a sermon every Sabbath in the kirk; teaches the school through the week; is agent for the Poor-Law Board, session-clerk, and registrar.*

GADA STACK—FOULA.

· Foula ·
f. Gaada Stack

*He makes first rate shoes and splendid coats, having originally
been a tailor by profession. He built his boat, he coopers, shoots,
fishes, farms his croft, and is a most successful sheep-farmer; for a
hardy breed of hungry sheep which he brought from Fair Isle have
multiplied very rapidly, to the alarm of the natives, who are afraid
lest they devour all the pasture on the 'scathold,' or commonty.*

And he had 14 children.

James Cheyne was born on Fair Isle and followed his father as
teacher there before taking the post on Foula in 1853. He was a
Society teacher, i.e. employed by the Society for the Propagation of
Christian Knowledge, which was brought to Shetland by the Established Church of Scotland at the beginning of the eighteenth
century to combat the 'abounding' superstition and ignorance 'ripe
for Roman Catholic conversion in the remoter islands'.

A FOULA COTTAGE.

JTR   *When in Foula I was particularly struck with the deep and honest religious sentiment which almost universally pervaded the people, and which was specially manifested in a profound attachment to the resident Independent preacher . . . The Foula men were wont to be a notoriously wild set of fellows; but the spirit of their dream is now changed, and in place of indulging in merry music and the dance, they are essentially a solemn people.*

The S.P.C.K. had obviously done its work well. Compared to Fair Isle, where Reid noticed at Sunday worship that the husbands of newly married couples quite openly 'waisted' their wives as they sat close together in the pews.

JTR   *Not long ago these islanders were much under the power of superstitious notions. One noted spirit, the "Nygel" or "Nigle" was supposed to appear near streams of running water, and particularly about water-mills, where, in the night, he seized and held fast the water wheel with his teeth until he was driven away by brands of fire thrown at him.*

A few old men told tales of a crossing to the mainland where '*a host of monsters*' rose out of the sea as if to devour them. '*These old Foula men still grow pale and become unnerved when they tell of that array . . .*'

And if you happened to see a circle of islanders throwing burning peats at a cow it was because '*the* trows *had taen the* quey *to the hills*' and they were getting her back.

The S.P.C.K. still had a lot of work to do.

I sensed *trows* and *nygels* and ghostly camera crews still abounded on Foula.

*   *   *

Like Margo and Bill on Fair Isle, my hosts Marion and Brian at Leraback had come to Foula in the '70s. The old thatched croft-house by the modern bungalow had been their first home. Both buildings and various outbuildings were perched above the tiny harbour and the *Haa* of Reid's time, then belonging to Scott of Melby, the owner of the island. The population was 233; 28 in 2010.

The island is split up into owner-occupied crofts and tenancies with no single landowner. The school had one pupil but three to come and one nursery child. The school is new and the size of a community hall, with freestanding banks of solar panels the length of the building. The digital keypad on the locked door took me aback.

Foula is a strange mix of new and old. At the harbour MV *New Advance* is lifted up onto its high concrete bed by massive cranes at the end of each return trip, no matter what the weather. Proof of how quickly conditions can change. Foula has had to fight hard for this provision.

And yet close by there are roofed ruins of what could have been a shop, a croft, long-left detritus spread round, and, saddest, a red rusted telephone box, the door fallen off, not worth local interest or

freight to a mainland museum or suburban garden. The dilapidation all the more poignant being so near to the modern community facility of the newly walled harbour. The *Clear Da Voes* and *Dinna Chuck Bruck* campaigns didn't seem to be working on Foula.

It was not for me to query such things, but there was an atmosphere on the island of stubborn neglect in reaction to Shetland Isles Council's equally stubborn lack of support.

But this butterfly had to avoid getting caught in any nets and get back to Mr Reid.

Loraback & Foula Harbour.

Haar lifting.

INTERIOR OF A FOULA COTTAGE.

JTR *In wet weather I spent many pleasant days in the Foula cottages, particularly* Leraback [the subject of the engraving 'A Foula Interior'] *and I ever found the inmates kind and polite. Leraback is a fair example of the Shetland cottage, and contains most of the articles of furniture peculiar to the country – the tall wooden press, long resting-chair or sofa, box-beds, anker-kettle,* daffach, *armchairs, and spinning wheels.*

In amongst all the engravings of headlands and islands and 'mansions' in *Art Rambles* there is this very detailed picture titled *Interior of a Foula Cottage*, which shows a domestic scene with two women, one spinning, the other possibly peeling a potato over a bowl, and a man with a pipe or a mug in his hand. All are seated. The fire smokes in the middle of the room. A dog lies on the floor.

'But that is our old crofthouse!' said the Taylors, in amazement. Three amazed people and Jess, the dog, aware of the excitement, went down the slope with the photocopied page and stood in the doorway of the old thatched cottage and looked into the selfsame

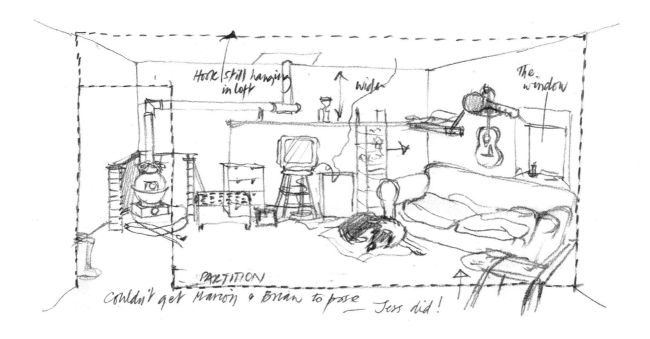

Interior of Leraback
Foula

interior, barring new partitions and false ceiling. Brian had recently started to modernise their old home. 'And the chain for the old fire in the middle of the room is still hanging from the roof ridge! Look!' Brian had lifted a hatch. And there in an unfinished adjoining room packed with furniture and boxes and cement bags, the resting-chair and wooden press. No doubt the kettle and the *daffach*, whatever that was, were in there, somewhere, too.

When I started sketching, Jess came in and curled up on the floor. Foula spirits came in the door with her.

*   *   *

Looming above everything on Foula are the mist-wreathed hills so like those of St Kilda, dropping a thousand feet perpendicular and more into the ever surging sea on the west of the island. The mist comes and goes with a life of its own. Reid climbed the Sneug and, fending off bonxies with the point of his sketching umbrella, narrowly escaped walking over the cliffs as many a Foula man had 'gone over'. The local euphemism not only meant spiritual trans-ference to God's Kingdom but also a literal demise on the rocks below. Powell uses the reference in the *Edge of the World* to symbolic effect.

I kept to the low ground of the north coast of the island to find yet another of Reid's headlands at Hiorawick. I'd been redrawing these too much. What was this obsession with headlands? A horizontal Victorian phallic need?

JTR   *On a Sabbath afternoon . . . a French fishing-vessel neared the island, from which the crew, having manned a boat, were seen to make for the coast, for the sad purpose of burying a much-loved shipmate. As the churchyard was at the other end of the island, and delay would endanger the safety of their vessel, the sad-hearted mariners, unwilling, nevertheless, to consign their companion to the keeping of the restless sea, buried him hurriedly at the top of one of the lonely cliffs pictured in the engraving of the 'North coast of Foula'.*

Apologies to Mr Reid and the French sailorman.

*   *   *

Big winds delayed the return flight to Tingwall. Waiting in the Taylor's stylish sitting room overlooking a steely grey frothed sea, the outsize TV showed me what was happening in the outside world. Where was that?

Out of the other window Marion was feeding toast to the tame bonxie.

My last memories of Foula.

CHAPTER VIII

Almost the Most Northerly
of the Most Northerly

In complete contrast to Foula is Whalsay. A not much larger island off the east coast of the mainland, it has a thirty-minute crossing and regular car ferry access from the marvellous road from Lerwick heading for the North Isles of Yell, Fetlar and Unst.

That was where Reid was wanting to get to from his base in Lerwick.

JTR   *. . . about noon, having got a glimpse of the rising sail of the* Imogen, *about to start for Unst, I made all haste to get on board . . . the tide proved stronger than the wind, as we vainly endeavoured to get through Whalsey Sound. Nought was left us but to anchor there for six hours. I took the opportunity of visiting Symbister, to enjoy a much and justly esteemed view from the door of the Ha' House – a splendid mansion, built of granite at the cost of £20,000. It is the residence of R. Bruce, Esq. of Symbister.*

Faithful to Reid's imposed detour I walked up to the grand elevation of Symbister House and can endorse his praises of its Georgian proportions, neoclassical stables, courtyards and panoramic view. The locals called it 'The Palace'.

By now I was getting familiar with the lifestyles and ambitions of nineteenth-century 'lairds' in Shetland, their rise and fall. The arc of Symbister was spectacular. Building started in 1820 and took 30 years to complete. The 5th Bruce laird, Robert Bruce, did not live long enough to see his extravaganza finished. In the interval he was ruthless with any men who went whaling to Greenland instead of fishing or labouring for him. Barbara Irvine, mother of two sons banished from Whalsay for whaling, placed a curse on the laird. 'A day would come, she swore, when there would be no Bruces left on Whalsay, the great mansion would stand empty and derelict with grass growing up between flagstones and local children would freely play in the grounds and courtyards.

By the 1920s the estate was bankrupt. The last Bruce laird died in 1944 with no male issue. Symbister House was bought by Shetland Isles Council in 1960 and is now the secondary school for Whalsay's population of over a thousand islanders. Predominately a modern fishing community, the crews and skippers own the huge pelagic trawlers based in Whalsay and, in reverse fashion, trade with the Hanseatic ports of Norway and Denmark.

True to the 'Laird's Curse', pupils were sitting and chatting in the sun outside Symbister House, younger ones tending rabbit pens on the lawn.

* * *

Reid finally got to Unst, landing at Uyea Sound and walking over the hills to Balta.

JTR *It was my good fortune while there to share, as so many had done before, the hospitable entertainment afforded by Thomas Edmondston, Esq., the generous laird of Buness.*

Edmondstons had held open house at Buness House for generations. A talented family of doctors and naturalists, their home was the meeting place for geologists, scientists and philosophers from all over Britain and Europe.

In amongst these brilliant men was a writer, Jessie Margaret Edmondston. Married to the ornithologist Henry Saxby by the time of her first publication, she is mentioned by Reid in his Introduction. '*The most recent work of general Shetland interest is a volume of poems,* 'Lichens from the Old Rock' *(1868) by Mrs Saxby, an accomplished islander, who very well appreciates the scenery of her native region, and loves its quaint customs and weird superstitions.*' Reid omits to tell that he did illustrations for her later stories for boys after meeting her at Buness, according to J. Laughton Johnston's *Victorians 60 Degrees North*.

Jessie M.E. Saxby went on to write more than 30 books in a range of other genres – novels, travel writing and journalism. Widowed early with small children, she became a writer 'by necessity' and an example of that talented and determined breed of

SKETCH OF TREES ON DR EDMONDSTON'S GROUNDS, BALTA SOUND, UNST.

— and Mrs Saxby ?

Victorian women. I wish Reid had met and mentioned more of them on his rambles. They would have been about.

A talented and determined Edmondston woman inhabits Buness today. Turning up at the many-starred Guest House sign on the imposing stone gate pillar, I parked the mature (rusty) Countess out of sight and crossed the lawn to where a tall gardener in blue overalls was working in a flower bed.

'Is it possible to speak to the owner?' I asked.

'In there,' indicated the gardener, nodding towards a large, tastefully decorated conservatory sitting room attached to the front of the old *Haa* overlooking Balta Sound. 'I'll tell her,' he said, and disappeared.

Eventually a querying and aproned Jennifer Edmondston came out into the garden. I explained my quest. She was terribly busy. 'A full house of guests. Come back next week, please.' A day and time was arranged. Another 'appointment' . . .

There was nothing for it but to get back to Reid's photocopied pages, stay in the area and plod on.

Balta Sound Hotel had the look of Sumburgh Hotel, though less grand. The central building could have been a Victorian manse but there were the telltale unbecoming extensions and chalets. A reminder of the boom days of 'the Oil'.

A bar supper was needed before steering the Countess to bed. 'Sorry,' said the barman in the lounge bar. It was 7 p.m. 'Try the public bar.'

'Sorry,' said the barman in the public bar, very apologetic. 'We've been told they are not available tonight. Crisps? Nuts?'

The bar was full of serious male drinkers. No, none of them could work out the location of Reid's sketch of Balta Sound. Perhaps the 'oilys' were back and only interested in the contents of their glasses.

The further north I travelled in Shetland, the more the premises advertised in the glossy brochures in the Tourist Office in Lerwick as offering evening meals – even a wine bar over at nearby Haroldswick – were shut.

It was June. It reminded me of the west coast of Scotland and its islands in the '70s. Not that I yearned for the superabundance of choice, B&Bs included, to be found there nowadays. That is not what I had come to Shetland for. In fact Shetland's low-key commercial tourism was a very pleasant and unpredicted surprise.

Try telling that to the islanders far from the honey pot of Lerwick who are trying to make a living from visiting *sooth moothers*. But I rest my case on those misleading advertisements.

The Countess found her bed. Not hidden up an old track or round the back of a deserted crofthouse – sites always picked for the view – but on the wide expansive headland of Lamba Ness that juts out into the vast expanse of the North Sea.

Here was World War II Britain's most northerly RAF Radar Station. It stretched the length and width of the headland and housed 150 men, with cinema and boxing ring and the office that published their *Outpost Magazine*; 15,000 tons of construction material made their concrete encampment.

Paths still connect the mossed-over foundations. Some roofless buildings still stand. The turfed pyramids that concealed equipment can be explored, water eerily dripping from lime-encrusted ceilings.

There was nothing depressing about the site despite a couple of grass-lined bomb craters. No one had been killed and the attack was never repeated. I looked out over the headland landscaped by latter-day flocks of sheep and imagined the men going about the chores and duties of their entrenched township, walking along the linking paths of a summer's day, looking at the view, stopping and standing still. Hearing the lapwings and larks high above, the endless wash and backwash of the waves below and writing home about it.

*   *   *

JTR *On a hill above the Bay of Haroldswick is a cairn of stones known as 'Harold's Grave' where search was recently made by scientific gentlemen for human remains. Their search was not unsuccessful, but many stones being thrown aside, we regretted that a time-honoured mound should have been thus disturbed, dispelling the mysterious interest that encircled these curious monuments.*

One wonders if the '*scientific gentlemen*' had anything to do with the visitors to Buness House over the hill.

Muckle Hoeg, the hill that Harold's reputed grave is atop, is over 450 feet high and gives a 180-degree clear sweep all the way to his homeland over the sea road to Norway. According to legend, Haroldswick is where the first Vikings landed on Shetland, but they

OLD ROUND-HEADED STONE CROSS, NORWICK, UNST.

To the
MARTIN
JAMES AN
"children

who die

love"
blooms so

The strange Crosses — Norwick . Unst.

were a troublesome lot and Harold, their king, came over himself to sort them out and stayed.

Long before the Vikings, prehistoric man had valued the vantage point. Big stone-work remains are still scattered over the top. A chambered cairn is marked on the map.

Whose bones were taken?

*   *   *

Other bones with safe, last resting places led Reid to Norwick, a couple of miles north of Haroldswick.

JTR *Having heard of several ancient stone-crosses in a churchyard in Norwick, I paid a visit to it one evening 'tween the gloamin' an' the mirk' . . . It was a wild spot, near the rock-bound Bay of Norwick. The crosses were almost buried among the weeds.*

They are there, these strange primitive, almost ugly, stone crosses, all of a few feet high, squat, bulbous and bearded with long strands of lichen. But not buried in weeds. The graveyards all over Shetland, even in the most remote spots far from present-day townships, are kept in meticulous condition. Close-mown grass and many with newly rebuilt pointed walls and trouble-free gates. 'Graveyards close to the sea,' explained an old man in Norwick. 'Easier to bring the bodies by boat in the old days.'

Norwick is a pretty little village close to its own beach. Houses are characterfully maintained and the classic upturned boat is roof to a large garage just by the graveyard. Further on up the most northerly road in Britain is the most northerly house at Skaw with the most northerly little beach just waiting for the most northerly picnic and swim. And another boat roof most northerly.

Thanks to the week's waiting time before going back to Buness House, I had plenty time to read and ramble.

In 1700, at Norwick, a sea eagle took a sleeping infant girl up in its talons and headed for its cliff nest. A local lad saw it happen and alerted the villagers and led them to the cliff top, where he was roped down and safely retrieved the baby. Of course they married when they both grew up and lived happily ever after – in Yell. Maybe no sea eagles in Yell.

A story ripe for one of Jessie Saxby's folklore books.

*   *   *

Reid had based himself at Buness House for his forays in Unst.

JTR   *Returning to Buness about midnight, I did not go to bed, but rested on the sofa for two hours, after which I left, without a guide, for the old castle of Muness, six or eight miles away. There was no road, and I had to find my way through a stony valley, strewn with boulders of every shape and size, all of a melancholy gray hue; while it required great care and circumspection to avoid sinking deep into occasional patches of quaggy soil. Before five I was seated on my camp-stool delineating a morning view of the ruins of Muness.*

Now there is dedication to one's art. And carrying the standard Brother Brush materials of '*a large sketching umbrella, a camp-stool, a waterproof case to hold a folio for drawings, fourteen inches by ten inches in size, and a small courier bag for the colour-box, a brush case, and a water flask*'.

Reid does admit to diminishing the full complement on occasion, packing his pockets with basics. But the camp-stool for himself and the umbrella for the bonxies were essential. For myself it was the wee rucksack with pencil, watercolour box, screw-top jam jar for water and a 'policeman's notebook'. Always room for the bar of chocolate, oatcakes, an apple and a map. Reid never mentions a map or food supplies in his knapsack. Sometimes there is reference to a guide but not for this trip to Muness.

I have a notion Reid would have travelled to Muness from Buness by going cross-county southwards and keeping the east coast in sight, for that is the direct route. The fine, main road streaking south down the middle of the island branches off left onto a minor road that ends at the headland of Mu Ness and the strategically placed castle.

Built in 1598 by Laurence Bruce, yet another member of the powerful Shetland family of Bruces, the castle was evidence of the power of a petty tyrant, according to Historic Scotland, but also of a man of 'exquisite taste'. The finished building, with two circular chambered tower rooms at diagonal corners, corbelling and little dormer windows, would have had the look of a French chateau. As ever there was not another soul about. The Historic Scotland sign said 'Castle Open. No Key Required'. Inside in the dim, cold stone-smelling corridor is a cupboard with torches for loan to explore the castle. Batteries fully topped up. I liked the touch.

*   *   *

It was easy for Reid to get from Muness to Fetlar.

JTR   *As soon as the fishermen were abroad I employed two of them to row me over to Fetlar. I have seldom enjoyed so pleasant a sail; it was quite a luxury to breathe on such a delightful morning. The Fetlar meadow-land is very fertile, but likewise sappy to such a degree that every step landed me in water over the shoes. Lead of varied hues, so soft that it can be cut out of the face of the cliffs with a knife, and easily fashioned into pencils before coming hard, is very abundant, but has never been turned to useful account. Asbestos, too, is found in considerable quantity; and, on the shore of one of the lochs, a deposit of magnetic sand is to be seen. I took a sketch of Brough Lodge, and accepted the invitation of Lady Nicolson, the proprietress, to lunch with her.*

The Countess and I had to backtrack to the main road and head for the Fetlar ferry from Belmont. Fetlar has long been called the Garden of Shetland. It *is* very fertile; Reid must have arrived after days of rain.

He also arrived after a lengthy period of troubled times and ruthless evictions. The Sir Arthur Nicolson of Kate's parentage and crossbreeding of sheep to graze that fertile land had died by the time Reid had lunch with his widow in the partly roofless Brough Lodge.

Arthur Nicolson was a Lerwick merchant who had travelled extensively in the East. Possibly this explains the Greco-roman–Gothic architecture of the lodge. He started building it in 1825, having gained Fetlar from one of those Bruces that owed him a debt. About the same time, he revived the title of Baronetcy of Nova Scotia given to the Nicolsons in 1629.

Sir Arthur also, with little regard to prehistory, built an astronomical Observatory Tower on top of a ruined broch behind the chapel and a summerhouse folly on the other side of the island. He spent his first and last night in the summerhouse when it was finished. It was a sleepless night; unaccountable noises kept him

MORNING SKETCH OF MUNESS CASTLE.

awake. It was the curses of the evicted tenants whose house stones had been taken for the construction of the folly.

Sir Arthur died childless, but Lady Nicolson had life rent of the property. The inheritor, in 1879, was the Australian grandson of a cousin of Sir Arthur's, another Sir Arthur, who did not take kindly to the condition of lodge and estate when he arrived. The lodge was roofless by then and the tenants complained bitterly about Lady Nicolson, who 'would not do anything for their comfort'. Some of them had refused to pay rent.

All in all, Fetlar was going through very difficult times when Reid visited. Did he know this? Was this why he lists all the mineral possibilities not capitalised?

Had the roof started to fall in completely? Her Ladyship spent most of the year in Cheltenham. Reid was lucky to get lunch.

*   *   *

Brough Lodge never recovered from that initial neglect and after many ensuing years of serious decay, Brough Lodge Trust has been created to save the historic building and develop it as a centre for Shetland arts activities, music study, performances and accommodation.

Muness Castle Unst.

Historic Scotland plan.

Muness Castle.
. Unst .

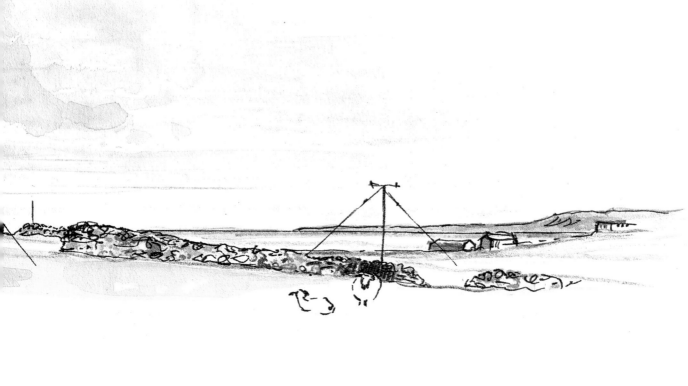

BROUGH LODGE—FETLAR.

From a population of 550 in 1861, the 70 islanders of 2010 are a 45 per cent increase on recent years and Fetlar looks to an enlivened future with no Nicolsons stargazing in the observatory. The lens of the telescope is in the Fetlar Interpretive Centre in amongst a wealth of Brough Lodge artefacts and photographs.

While I was there the annual *Foy* was being celebrated, with marquees and barbecues down by the beach and campsite at Tresta. Long into the *simmer dim* night, the local bands kept the oyster-catchers silent. The Countess and I were parked round the side of the chapel at deserted Brough Lodge, the Nicolson motto 'Generositate' inscribed somewhere up on the masonry behind us.

*   *   *

It was time to head back northwards for 'the appointment' at Buness House. Then to '. . . *gain the extremity of Hermaness – to sketch the "Muckle Flugga Lighthouse" and "Out-Stack", the most northerly rock in the British Isles . . .*' This would be my last re-enactment of Reid's *Art Rambles in Shetland*.

It had been two months of freedom and fatigue, delight and doubt, but most rewarding of all, an insight not only into my time in Shetland but also that of Reid. Getting off the ferry at Toft, I could not resist a last 'burn' down that marvellous road to the Archives at Hay's Dock in Lerwick for a final indulgent immersion

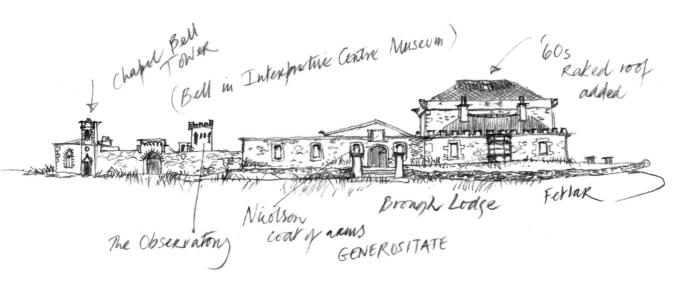

Chapel Bell Tower

(Bell in Interpretive Centre Museum)

'60s Raked roof added

The Observatory

Nicolson coat of arms GENEROSITATE

Brough Lodge

Fetlar

in nineteenth-century Shetland.

How is it created, that hallowed atmosphere of archive departments? The almost imperceptible hum of humidifiers, air conditioners and computers? The soft-shoed tread of soft-spoken staff? One's own aura, and that of everyone else, intense with silent purpose?

Added to the ranks of microfilms, forms and fiches that will give 'the answer', I like to think the old books, manuscripts, prints and maps add and seep their own dust-flavoured essence into the mix.

It was a busy time of year for the archive department and the atmosphere was purposeful and not very silent. The *hamefarers* were there in force.

How admirably patient were the staff, listening to the spread of wide branched family trees. And so understandable, the passionate recounting of dates and details by the descendants. Usually couples with one partner's family the focus of the detective work. The other partner had heard it all before, I could tell. How gently, but firmly,

the staff would steer the *hamefarer* away from dead end or lopped off branches.

One elderly Australian, wheelchair-bound and tubed, wheeled back and forth to the archivist's desk in a delirium of excitement. The oxygen in his tube gurgling. To be so ill, to have travelled so far, to find out that his forebears had existed and lived in actual places in Shetland that could be pointed out on the map made everything so worthwhile.

The human spirit has deep roots.

*   *   *

Farewells to Hay's Dock and the road north once more.

Passing the West Mainland junction, I noticed a sign for a Village Hall Tea in Tingwall. Village Hall Teas are legend in Shetland. Of a Saturday afternoon communities will host a cream-laden cornucopia of home baking in their decorated Village Hall for

Brough Lodge - looking to Mainland
Fetlar

local funds. Islanders travel from all over to test and taste the competition. Cruise ships are unreliable.

I turned back. The event was a fundraiser for the Shetland ex-Whalers' Association to get a plaque made for display on Lerwick pier.

All of the world of Shetland and his wife were sitting at the packed tables the length of the hall. Around the walls were photographs from the whaling eras of Shetland, Greenland and South Georgia; people moving slowly round to look at the whalers and their ships as in a queue in a Tate Gallery exhibition. In a side room were black-and-white grainy films of crow's nests and bow harpoons and mast-high waves, open bridges and woollen mittens crusted in ice.

With my plate of trawled sandwiches, biscuits and 'fancies', I sat down beside Hugh. He was proud to tell me that there were over a hundred ex-whalers still living in Shetland and he was one of them. They often met and this year they had the idea to collect money for a plaque. 'You know, there is no public record of that time in Shetland life. We've raised £7,000 so far.'

Aged 17 in 1943, Hugh had joined the Pioneers. Recovering from a burst appendix that affected his health, he was sent to Burma with the Army Catering Corps. This he survived to come back to Shetland and then join the Antarctic whaling fleet in '48.

Whaling had been part of Shetland life for generations, but those generations had fished them out of the Atlantic. In 1845, the biggest Atlantic catch of 1,540 was recorded in Shetland. The last whaling station at Olna was closed in 1929.

The industry followed the whales to Antarctica and so did the Shetland men valued for their traditional skills. This was an accepted way of life; it was just a bit further from home. Employed by Salveson, Hugh was sent to the Leith Whaling Station in South Georgia. First time he tagged on with Shetlanders already employed. 'If they liked the look of your face, you were taken on.'

There were 800 men working in the summer whaling season based in South Georgia; 300 serviced the plant in winter and over the year 200 maintained the 'catcher' boats.

Conditions were appalling. 'We slept in sheds and lived in ordinary clothes and oilskins. Sweat froze inside on your back. And despite the cold temperatures we were afflicted with burrowing bugs that affected our nerves. Very painful. It was always my neck but the pain could be all over your body.'

Hugh got the back of his hand accidentally caught on a harpoon. 'The doctor was no use and it was just bandaged up. I got on with the work as best I could.' Back home at the end of the season, he was sent to an Edinburgh hospital. 'But it was too late. The two bones had grown together.'

There were good times, as witnessed in the photos around the hall. 'We got a tot of rum once a month but we made many a brew out of anything we could get our hands on. Whale meat was delicious.'

Antarctic whaling ceased in 1963. A way of life was gone for ever.

The Village Hall hummed with camaraderie and nostalgia. Teenagers mixed easily with adults as they do in small communities. It was their grandfathers' and great grandfathers' day and the stories would be familiar to them.

Shetlanders have a strong sense of identity. Islanded so far north of mainstream Britain, they keep the history of their communities alive and well. That separateness from Scotland, despite modern communication links and social mobility, is in the air all around. They have survived so much in recent history – the landlords and their sheep, industrial exploitation, starvation, emigration. This was happening elsewhere, of course. The Highlands and Islands primarily. But there is a sad residual *ochone! ochone!* still to be heard weaving in and out of the croft ruins in the west. Somehow the Shetlanders got up and got on with it.

Before I left, Hugh was keen to tell me that for all the tall stories about whales the biggest ever was caught off Shetland. 'And with a gun much lighter than those used in South Georgia.'

I got him another cup of tea and left a donation in the box.

*   *   *

The *haar* had clung to the land for several days, reluctantly lifting by late afternoon. No sun-splintered waves would be crashing over Muckle Flugga for my last image of Shetland. But it made sense to get there with time in hand for a change in the weather and the lengthy walk of the Burra Firth. Best to forget Buness House? I so nearly did. But an 'appointment' is an appointment.

Knocking several times at the open side door, there was no reply.

Tentatively calling and entering what would have been the original seventeenth-century *Haa,* the stone flagged floor led my stockinged feet silently on to the 1828 extension, built by the then laird, Dr Edmondson, to accommodate the views over Balta Sound and onto which the spacious conservatory was now attached.

This was the house that all those famous nineteenth-century scientists, naturalists and academics had visited. Lady Franklin had stayed in 1849 whilst obsessively endeavouring to get news of her explorer husband who never returned from his attempt to navigate the Northwest Passage in the Arctic. She quizzed locally returned whalers to no avail; but got them to take her to Out Stack beyond Muckle Flugga with the intention of landing on it, but the crew advised against this. She was allowed to touch the seaweed-draped rock that was the nearest part of Britain to the Arctic and commune with Lord Franklin, dead or alive.

The house was silent. Where were my present-day hosts? And you and your ghosts, Mr Reid?

By the time I got to the dining room, I was feeling very uncomfortable. I looked at my watch. I did have the day and the time correct. That awful decision to turn round and leave but maybe be caught creeping out from the very heart of someone's home . . . for that was the feel of the place even although its four public stars are extensively advertised. The old, grand house furnishings and colonial relics are all in keeping with the history of the house, the big vases of summer flowers on shining deep mahogany tables and sideboards, placed with a stylish eye. There were no reproductions here or whimsical IKEA additions and yet it was not a museum.

A door opened, light flooding in from a large kitchen. 'Ah, you're here! Thought we heard something. Come into the conservatory.' It was the gardener, without the overalls.

David and Jennifer Edmondston have been 'hosting' at Buness House for 15 years. The inheritance of the complicated Edmondston estate had burdens and I got the impression that the 'hosting' was the lesser of many evils. Or maybe it was the greater. Latterly Jennifer has been doing the cooking and housekeeping herself. Exhaustion was setting in.

But both of them had time and genuine, if slightly offhand, interest in my project until I showed them the photocopies of Reid's book and his comments on the generosity of David's forbear and the engraving of Buness House. It was as if the house around us breathed easy and had come into its own again and was peopled with all its gifted ghosts instead of twentieth-century B&B holiday-makers and passers-by.

'Buness and Sandlodge are the only two properties left that have hereditary family residents,' rued Jennifer as she handed over coffee and chocolate biscuits. I thought it best not to mention Raewick.

David had quietly left the room. I stroked the ancient, long-haired tabby on one of the flower-cushioned wicker chairs and thought of my ginger boys waiting at home.

'What was his name again? The artist?' David had come back with a curved piece of old cardboard about 14 by 24 inches in size. Its edges were worm-holed. On one side was a watercolour painting of the exact view of Buness as in Reid's engraving. He turned it over. On the back was a signature – John T. Reid. The cat jumped off the chair.

Jennifer was as amazed as I.

I was actually looking at a Reid watercolour.

Of course, he would have given a finished painting as a token of thanks, here and there, as he rambled on. The original sketches, like my own, would be worked on later at home. Reid would then transfer the images by drawing in line onto a block of wood for the engraving process.

And I was *here* and could have been *there*, walking to Muckle Flugga . . .

The artwork was not true watercolour. There was a tad too much white pigment, as though Reid would rather have been working in oils. Tidy, competent, with detailed study and execution of the stones of the boulder-strewn foreground, I could only fault him on the blue blueness of his sea. Like sunsets, it is a colour trap I fall into myself.

David had disappeared again. This time, like the proverbial magician, he brought in a gold-framed painting from the dark recesses of the house.

'Been on the wall for years. Didn't know anything about it,' he said, bemused. The subject, stone for stone and wave for wave, was the original of the engraving of the French sailor's headland on Foula.

I look back now and am amazed that I did not ask to buy at least one of the paintings, but the thought never even crossed my mind as I sat there shocked at the memory of the decision, oh! so

BALTA SOUND—UNST.

John T. Reid original with Buness House, centre left

NORTH COAST OF FOULA.

John T. Reid original

nearly taken, to drive on past Buness House.

Just to have seen those originals and know that they exist and are where they rightly belong is enough.

*   *   *

A kind of 'mission accomplished' mood came upon me. Did I really need to go to Muckle Flugga? Just another lighthouse, and of no importance to me that it is the most northerly part of Britain. I had no Lord Franklin to commune with and I had had my fill of bonxies.

But it would have been churlish to desert Mr Reid on the last few pages.

Buness
· Balta Sound ·   Unst ·

CHAPTER IX

A Moderately Lengthy Introduction to the End

JTR *To gain the extremity of Hermaness – to sketch the 'Muckle Flugga Lighthouse' and 'Out-stack', the most northerly rock in the British Isles – proved exhausting work, as it is no easy task in warm weather to travel up such heights and down such dales as are to be found in Shetland . . .* [The lighthouse] *can only be reached at one point, and that in very calm weather, by steps cut out of the solid rock. The life of those lonely light-keepers must be monotonous enough. The storm of 24th January, 1868 was felt there with tremendous force; and when I visited it last July, labourers were still employed repairing the damage done that dreadful night, when they were in instant expectation that the lighthouse would be swept away. The waves of the North Sea were breaking over it, although the rock on which it is built is two hundred feet in height, and the light-room stands sixty feet higher. Their quarters were snug, though small; their walls papered, and the floor carpeted with pictures from the* Illustrated London News. *Three of them at a time dwell in this ocean-home, while a fourth is on shore, where comfortable houses have been erected for the wives and families of the light-keepers; and on entering which, I found them models of tidiness, contrasting forcibly with the native huts.*

Well, there you go, Mr Reid; build decent housing for your workers and miracles can happen.

The Muckle Flugga shore station was safely tucked into the west shore of the narrow Burra Firth at Ness and one of the few accommodation blocks built separate from its lighthouse. The narrow serrated ridge formation of the sea-girt rocks that make up the collective name of Muckle Flugga had just enough space for the lighthouse tower and its surrounding protective yard wall.

It was commissioned by the UK Government at the time of the

Crimean War. Safe navigation round the north of Scotland was of paramount importance. Muckle Flugga must have been a challenge on a par with Skerryvore in the Hebrides built ten years previously in 1844 by the Stevenson brothers.

Thomas, R.L. Stevenson's father, was engineer in charge at Muckle Flugga and employed a hundred men in its construction. The building materials were shipped from the little port at Ness and once the station was built the lighthouse and its keepers were serviced from there by the Northern Lighthouse Board.

The base for the foundations had to be quarried down into the rock to a depth of ten feet before building the tower. The first light-house, built in 1854, was 50 feet high but proved unsatisfactory in the winter storms. Waves burst open the entrance door and flooded the base of the building. A further 16 feet were added to the overall height on the second attempt. By 1858, the lighthouse was finished and lit.

A Muckle Flugga toll, by Government order, of one penny per ton was levied on British ships and any foreign vessels that used British ports passing Muckle Flugga.

By 1853, the light was 'illuminated' by an electro-magnetic system but there was no modernisation of the keepers' environment. 'We slept in a crow's nest and ate in a cell,' the principal keeper was reputed to have said. Once modern electrification was installed in 1969 there was more room in the yard and an on-site dwelling block was built.

Muckle Flugga was automated in 1995 and the shore station was sold to Scottish Natural Heritage to become the Visitor Centre for their Hermaness Nature Reserve. The Reserve stretches from the road end car park to the extremity of the headland and a precipitous view of the lighthouse, onto which 200-foot waves still land fish on its doorstep.

R.L.S. visited his father's lighthouse in 1869. Tourist brochures claim that Unst was the inspiration for *Treasure Island*. He signed the visitors' book in the lighthouse and must have clambered up the slippery rock before Reid's visit in the same year. There is no comment in *Art Rambles*, surprisingly. The two young men were artists and writers living in Edinburgh and of a similar age; R.L.S. was 19 years old and Reid about 23 years old in 1869. It would be a further 14 years, however, before Stevenson became famous on the publication of *Treasure Island*.

But maybe Reid didn't thumb through or sign visitors' books. A man after my own heart in that regard.

*   *   *

My last rambling day started with a light warm haze, no *haar*. But there was a sharpness in the little wind that nipped the bridge of my nose. A good day for a long walk. The Countess and I had spent the previous night on a track by the side of Loch of Cliff and woke to ducks squabbling in the reeds.

I remembered how the domestic ducks and hens had to be kept in pens in Foula for fear of predation by the Great Skua. Today I would be heading into their silent province at Hermaness – the Land of the Pirate Bonxie. Bonxies chase and harass other birds in flight to get them to disgorge their food. Perhaps it is true that R.L.S. did base *Treasure Island* on Unst.

Shetland is the world's main breeding location of the bird. It is fitting that the local name is now universal. In 1831, there were only three pairs of the Great Skua at Hermaness. They were thought to be the only ones in Britain except for the small colony on Foula. Dr Laurence Edmondston, of that 'talented' family at Buness, led the campaign with Scott of Melby to save the birds and by 1850 the population had risen to 50 pairs. There are now about 700 pairs. And this was the breeding season. I looked for a stick in the scrubby little wood by the loch.

The narrow winding road contours along the side of the Firth to the Hermaness Nature Reserve. At the road end is the *ultima Thule* of all car parks, which is in two sections; one at the Visitor Centre by the jetty, the other up the hill at the gated entrance to the reserve.

I counted 251 vehicles – from campervans to a topless two-seater tourer, cars, motor and pedal cycles in between. So *this* is where everybody goes, I thought. It was only mid morning. The loudspeaker on the charter boat at the jetty was advising the queuing rucksacked, camera- and binocular-bedecked mariners the dos and don'ts of Health and Safety for their sail round Muckle Flugga.

Mousa memories. But no one would be allowed to land on the lighthouse island.

I packed my little rucksack, not ashamed of my misanthropic decision, and set off through the gate and onto the well-worn uphill track. On the first stretch turns were politely taken to step to the side with returning walkers who had completed the way-marked circuit – or had done as much as they could or would.

At the top, the track became boarded for great stretches of the moor, signifying lethal peat hags in wet weather. Figures dotted the landscape almost as much as the bog cotton. A woman walked past with a bag that had fronds of bracken and fern sticking out of it. The bag was environmentally hessian with a green logo on its side, but I don't think samples of the *Dennstaedtiaceae* family are appropriate plunder on a nature reserve no matter how green the logo.

The male bonxies were benign and stood tall-legged, hardly budging as long as I kept to the path. With all the traffic, they had become quite streetwise. Mating for life, they diligently protected the nesting females, as black brown as are their nests in the distant peat hags.

Halfway to Hermaness Hill the bog cotton thinned, as did the walkers. Most were heading back and the slow, long climb led to welcome desolation and a terrain shaved by winter winds. Old scattered stones at the top from a lookout tower of not that long ago gave shelter from the updraught of a chill little summer wind. And far below, the line of the dragon's spine of jagged rocks encircled by deceptively benign breaking waves leading to the larger fin of rock on which the lighthouse stood. It looked so small and insignificant!

In contrast to this diminutive view and silence of the blanket bog left far behind, the cackling, screaming cacophony of 17,000 pairs of breeding gannets lifting up from the white guano-washed rocks was like an explosion of aural shrapnel.

The track ends halfway down the steep grassy slope and wisely I went no further to get a closer look at the lighthouse. It would be a longer slip than the one at Kirstan's Hole in Papa Stour, but the end result would be the same.

Gaining the top of Hermaness again for a last look out across the endless wave-flecked table of the sea, precipitation veiling the horizon line endless miles north, I then looked over to Saxa Vord to the east, bristling with radio masts, on the other side of the Burra Firth.

Long, long ago a giant lived there, right on the *vord* top, and he was called Saxa. Here on the top of Hermaness Hill lived another giant. He was called Hermann. The giants were sworn enemies because they both loved and fiercely quarrelled over a beautiful mermaid that would sit on the Muckle Flugga rock and tantalisingly comb her long, long tresses.

They would throw colossal boulders, which to them would be but pebbles, across the Firth, aiming to kill the other. Being clumsy and overweight, they kept missing their mark and the boulders fell into the sea and became the great rocks at the foot of each headland. In their crazy battle one boulder ended up far out to sea and that became Out Stack, the nearest rock to the northern edge of the world.

The mermaid got fed up with their behaviour and said she would marry the giant that would swim all the way with her to the North Pole. Immediately they dived down from the top of their

No Reid engraving for this
 pity —

respective hills into the sea – and drowned.

There is something not quite right about that story. I think it is the mermaid. Culturally she doesn't fit into Shetland sea mythology – or Hebridean, although the Gaelic *ceasg* means maid of the sea.

A mermaid is not a shapeshifter. Worldwide she is always the same; a human torso with a fish's tail. Likewise her merman counterpart, but he does not have much interest in humans. Most likely because it was only fishermen that were capable of sighting a merman.

Essentially a mermaid lures her victims into the sea and there they drown. Some say she doesn't know that humans have to breath air and is innocent. I have my doubts about the Muckle Flugga one.

e Flugga' and the
Most Northerly Bonxie

Selkies, on the other hand, are never wicked. Just look at their eyes. They are never provocative. They only take their skins off for their own private enjoyment of a moonlit night on a beach. The fisherman who sees and captures one in her human form hides her sealskin, for that is the only way he can keep her. They should live happily ever after, for seals in human form are always beautiful and gentle.

But she, compliant and dutiful as a wife should be, can still be found of a moonlit night down by the shore, lamenting her entrapment. We want her to find her skin despite the undoubted love she and the fisherman have for each other and their human children. When she finds it, as must be, we swim away with her into the far deep to be with her own kind who have always been waiting for her.

And hope that the fisherman will find one of his own kind to look after all those children. But that is the scenario for another kind of folktale.

The best *selkie* folktale I came across on Shetland was from Papa Stour. I like it because the story is told from the deserted bull seal's point of view.

Papa men were out fishing by the Ve Skerries when a freak storm arose and one of the men fell overboard and was swept towards the rocks. Hermann, for that was his name, pulled himself to safety on the skerries, but the men could not get the boat close enough to enable him to jump back on board. The boat made for home, his comrades calling through the roar of the storm that they would come back for him when the weather had calmed.

Soon his comrades were out of sight and Hermann prepared for a wet and uncomfortable night. At this point a bull seal raised its head from the turbulent waves and asked Hermann for a favour.

'My wife was taken by one of your islanders from the beach at Housa Voe. I hear her plaintive song every full moon. I know where her skin is hidden. If I take you back home, will you get it for me?'

'Of course,' said Hermann.

'Take your knife and cut a foothold on each side of my body then hang on tight round my neck.' And so saying, man and *selkie* swam fast and effortlessly through the storm waves to Papa Stour.

The *selkie* told Hermann which shed and in which barrel his wife's skin had been hidden.

It was near midnight by the time the other fishermen arrived back to the island, safe but exhausted and afeared of telling what had happened to Hermann. But when they got to his house there he was sitting by the fire warm, cosy and dry.

It is not told which of the men went back to his house that stormy night to find his bairns motherless. But it is a well-known fact that a Papa Stour man would never harm a seal.

Many years later when Hermann was a very old man, he found a dead bull seal washed up on the beach of Housa Voe. On each side of its body were scars the length of a foothold.

I will let Mr Reid have the last confusing word on the matter of mermaids and *selkies*.

JTR *Papa Stour . . . is rich in legends . . . the 'Vae Skerries,' which lie out therefrom at a distance of some miles . . . are the haunt of seals, which are called* selkies *in Shetland, and which, according to popular belief, were mermen and mermaids in disguise. At night they disrobed themselves of their seal-skins, and, boasting forms beautiful beyond description, held their midnight revels in the pale moonlight, amid the surges that broke over these skerries. Many wonderful stories are told about them: they are said to have carried shipwrecked fishermen on their backs safe to the shore of Papa.*

*   *   *

The walk back from the headland was on a welcome decline. The few late walkers were miles ahead, disappearing down the final slope to the car park. The day's warm haze had turned to trailing fingers of muslin fog. The windless air carried the melancholy call of a golden plover, the drumming vibration of snipe. I had the last of the moor and the last of Shetland to myself. Reid had been left behind at Buness.

*   *   *

On the way back to Lerwick next day to catch the evening sailing to Aberdeen I called at the Plantiecrub Garden Centre near Tingwall airport. The name had intrigued me on first sighting. I had learned it was the Shetland word for the many small circular walled enclosures of land dotted all over the more remote parts of Shetland. Except for affluent Whalsay, where there were many up on the hill over to Skaw, but it was the prevalence of trampolines with identical dimensions outside nearly every house that caught my eye on that island.

Planticrubs, or *plantie-cruives* according to Reid, were shelters for growing kale; safe from sheep and, being completely round, safe from the direct full force of the wind. None are used now but of those still intact some have naturalised shrubs and little trees growing inside that give them the look of pretty, drystane flower bowls that Hermann and Saxa would have as table decorations.

The Plantiecrub Garden Centre is the most northerly garden centre in Britain. For all my snide comment on all things 'most northerly', here I was looking for a plant to take home from that very latitude. I chose two pots of thrift. Sea pinks to Coll!

*   *   *

Nearly a year has passed and they have transplanted fine and flower beside their Hebridean cousins. They remind me of the drifts of sea pinks on the Ness of Hillswick and *idder plices fir by.*

"THE DRONGS"—FROM THE POINT OF HILLSWICK NESS.

The last cliff walk

Glossary

auld – old

awa' fra dis toon – get away from here

böd – fishing hut/store

busses – deep sea Dutch fishing boats, nineteenth century

bonxie – Great Skua gull

Caain' Whales – Pilot Whales

clear da voes – clear/clean the sea inlets

da Grind – the Gate

da haaf – the offshore fishing grounds/open sea

da street – the street

dinna chuck bruck – don't throw/leave rubbish

foy – celebration

geo – inlet in cliffs

haa – big house, laird's house

haar – sea mist

hamefarin – homecoming

holm – small uninhabited grassy island

idder plices fir by – other places as well

ladeberry/lodberrie – enclosed wharf

lodberry – Lerwick house built into the sea

mirk – dark

moorit – brown sheep's wool

muckle – big

nae faat – no bother

peerie – small

plantie-cruive/planticrub – round-walled enclosure for growing
    kale/cabbage

pund – walled animal enclosure

quey – heifer/young cow

roost – strong current or tide

scathold – common grazing

scories/skorie – young seagull
selkie – seal
shelties – Shetland ponies
siller – money
simmer dim – summer twilight
sixareens – six-oared boats
skul –school
smooriekins – kisses
sooth moother – a southerner
trowie – night elf/imp
Up Helly Aa – fire festival (*helly* – holiday)
voe – sea inlet
vord – hill

Bibliography

The Isle of Foula, Ian B. Stoughton Holbourn (Birlinn)

Local News, Life in Shetland as Reported in the Provincial Newspapers, Volume I, The Emigration Years 1862–1881, compiled and edited by Malcolm Hulme (The Shetland Times Ltd)

Shetland, A Love Story: Letters of Robert Jamieson and Barbara Laing, edited by Kay Wheatcroft (The Shetland Times Ltd)

Travels in Shetland 1832–1852, Edward Charlton (The Shetland Times Ltd)

Two Calves in the House: Shetland Journal of Rev. John Lewis, edited by Harold R. Bowes (The Shetland Times Ltd)

Victorians 60 Degrees North, J. Laughton Johnston (The Shetland Times Ltd)

Wast Wi Da Valkyries, Christine De Luca (The Shetland Library, 1997)

With Naught But Kin Behind Them, Norah Kendall (The Shetland Times Ltd)